501 Gardening Tips

Other books by Pamela Donald
published by Piatkus

1001 Supersavers
501 DIY Supersavers

501 Gardening Tips

*Hints and tips to save you time
and money*

Pamela Donald

PIATKUS

Copyright © Pamela Donald 1991

First published in 1991 by
Judy Piatkus (Publishers) Limited,
5 Windmill Street, London W1P 1HF

The moral right of the author has been asserted

A catalogue record for this book is available
from the British Library

ISBN 0–7499–1104–2

Cover design and illustration by Ken Leeder
Cartoons by Ron McTrusty
Illustrations by Zena Flax

Typeset by Phoenix Photosetting, Chatham, Kent
Printed and bound in Great Britain by
Mackays of Chatham PLC, Chatham, Kent

Contents

Introduction

I believe some people really do have the god-given ability to make gardens flourish where others have failed, and copying their sometimes bizarre tips and old wives' remedies produced amazing results for me too.

I have known at least two women who loved their plants and gardens so much that the plants seemed to sense it and respond. First there was my mother. Many years ago we moved to a house near the banks of the Tay in Dundee, where despite the previous occupiers' clinical approach to the tending of the many varieties which grew there, neat, tidy, weed and fungus free, the garden was unremarkable.

An obsessive gardener, my mother had only one book on the subject, a treasured autographed copy of one of his manuals, given to her by the late Percy Thrower. I'm sure she knew every word by heart. But most of her talent for growing things owed much to ancient gardeners' lore and Scots' thrift – she always carried in her handbag small plastic bags, rubber bands and sharp scissors. Cuttings collected on her travels would emerge from the cluttered bag and unfailingly set down roots and live happily ever after. Her newly acquired, hitherto lacklustre garden soon blossomed into a mini paradise of scents and colours and was where she was happiest.

Years later, when I lived in the Arabian Gulf, I met a Dutch florist, Ann Van Benthem, who opened the first shop in Abu Dhabi selling flowers and plants. She, too, taught me much about caring for plants as living things and not merely as decorative or edible objects. Many of her tips are included here. They often relate to considering the feelings of plants and talking to them – which people may consider barmy, but which does seem to work!

In case this sounds like an all-female gardeners' club, I am always grateful to gardening expert and author Jock McGregor who showed me the best ever way to re-pot plants and many other time-saving tricks which he'd learned during his years as a top nurseryman.

When choosing 501 tips, I discarded those which I felt had a limited appeal. For instance, I came across one for stopping deer eating trees by wrapping creosoted rags round the bark. What sort of gardener would find a use for that, I wondered?

A few days ago I received my answer. My manuscript completed, I moved to a new home, where I am lucky enough to have acres of garden, orchard and the challenge of an established vineyard to care for. On the first evening, I gazed out in total contentment at the view from the kitchen window. Across the lawn tiptoed a beautiful fawn, and we watched spellbound as he purposefully headed for the rose bed and began feasting on buds and shoots, stripping a whole bush in seconds before scampering off at great speed!

I'm often asked if I try all the tips I come across. My eccentric rose trees festooned with smelly rags are the latest proof that I most surely do try.

Pamela Donald
Corner House Vineyard
Hendred
Oxfordshire

Garden Equipment

1. Plastic Squash bottles with their bottoms cut off, act as minicloches for young plants like courgettes or lettuces. Push them well into the ground to protect them from cutworms and slugs. Later, unscrew the tops to acclimatise the plants to colder air.

2. Old stockings or tights, the more laddered the better, are just the thing for storing bulbs. Hang them in a cool, dry place. You can store a glut of onions in this way too.

3. Cut up old stockings or tights in strips to make useful ties for garden and greenhouse plants. Because they stretch, they won't restrict growth.

4. Old potato peelers make useful gadgets for removing weeds from a lawn.

5 Collect plastic screw top containers to store a winter supply of herbs. Gather parsley, mint, rosemary, thyme etc, when at the peak of their freshness. Put the herbs on a baking tray in a cool oven until they are dry enough to be broken up into small pieces by gentle rubbing. Mushrooms can be dried in the same way.

6 Plastic food containers – yoghurt, cottage cheese tubs etc, with drainage holes punched in the bottom – are as good as shop-bought plastic flower pots for cuttings.

7 Construct a makeshift greenhouse for early planting, with heavy duty polythene attached to stout canes and placed at an angle against a sheltered wall.

8 Don't buy supporting canes for young plants. Use lengths of twigs and branches, which will look less conspicuous as the plants grow through them.

9 To grow DIY bamboo canes you need a fair amount of garden space as the shrub-like grasses will grow to about 10 feet (3m) tall. But they are less expensive and not too difficult to grow, and make attractive screens in not-too-exposed conditions. Harvest in the autumn, store flat, or hang up in bunches with twine and keep in a cool place to ensure straight, even drying.

10   A pair of gardening gloves will give longer service if spare left-hand ones are washed and turned inside out (the right handed one generally wears out first, unless of course you are left-handed). When finished with, rubber gardening gloves can make tough elastic bands, by cutting strips from the wrists and fingers.

11   Mend a garden hose with an off-cut of copper piping. Cut out the damaged part, immerse the newly cut ends in hot water to stretch them, and insert the piping to fill the gap.

12   Once your garden hose has too many holes in it to make it repairable, add a few more and turn it into a sprinkler for lawn or vegetable patch.

13   Recycle unwanted wire bicycle baskets. Line, fill with compost and flowering plants, and attach to an outside wall for a spring and summer display.

14   Save lengths of old guttering. Simply drill small holes in the bottom for easy watering of vegetable patches. Lay the guttering alongside each row of vegetables, then pour a bucket of water in one end.

15   Where you have shallow, heavy, or badly drained soil, raised beds to which you add bulky organic matter are an excellent investment. One of the simplest ways to contain the added soil is with railway sleepers, for which corner supports are unnecessary. Worth comparing the price with the alternative for the job – gravel boards and pegs. Ask sleeper merchants (Yellow Pages) for details.

16 In these ecologically minded times, there is no cheap substitute for a shredder, but the purchase of one (often to be found through second hand columns in gardening magazines) will pay handsome dividends. You can chop up all sorts of goodies for mulching and compost, and dispense with the need for anti-social, environmentally unfriendly bonfires.

17 Save money and the environment by substituting recycled paper pots for the peat variety when potting. Use the bottom of a bottle to mould broad strips of newspaper (using a thin flour and water paste will aid their adhesion) into a pot shape and let them dry thoroughly to weld into sturdy enough containers for planting. They will disintegrate and feed the soil when placed in the ground later.

18 Broken flower pots and crockery can still serve a useful purpose. Smash them into small pieces and use them to line the bottom of plant pots for good drainage.

Planting and Tending

Soil, Compost and Fertilisers

19 Conserving as much goodness in the soil as you can makes it unnecessary to spend on additives to improve tired plants. Mulching with organic matter – grass cuttings, leaf litter, well rotted farmyard manure etc – retains moisture in the soil. Keeping the plots well dug and aerated helps roots spread more easily. Placing windbreaks around beds will cut down the drying effect of wind. Removing weeds as soon as they appear stops them robbing plants of vital supplies of nutrients and water, and planting seedlings well apart so they don't have to fight with their neighbours for a share of food and drink is all to the good.

20 Human and animal hair thrown on the compost heap adds a valuable source of trace elements. Before modern pesticides, hair would be placed in the bottom of a bean trench to entangle hungry beasties intent on destroying the pods as they were laid.

21 Instead of spending money on soil testing kits, give yourself a free estimate from the weeds which grow on it. Chickweed thrives on rich soil with good drainage, docks and poppies prefer acid soil, and an abundance of moss on wet soil is bad news; the drainage is poor and will need lime added before planting. Ask a professional at your local garden centre to advise.

22 Only use organic compost from your waste – grass mowings, nettles, kitchen refuse etc. Crumpled pieces of wet newspaper placed under new plants as they are put in the ground helps to retain water and supply nutrients.

23 Mulching preserves the condition of the soil at the particular time you apply it. This is why you should never mulch soil when it's very wet, extra cold, or very dry. Planting and mulching spring-warmed soil gives good results.

24 Nettles speed up the decomposing process of a compost heap. If young fruit trees or bushes are planted in the spot where nettles have been dug up, they'll have instant enriched nursery beds.

25 Lime may be needed in areas where the soil is of a peaty, acid type, or just in a generally undernourished condition. The golden rule is to apply it (spring or autumn) a month before planting and 2 or 3 months after manuring, because lime and manure can never be applied at the same time.

26 After Twelfth Night your rootless Christmas tree can begin the first day of the rest of its life. Remove its side branches (and pass them through a shredder) leaving the trunk to make a sturdy support for climbers such as roses and clematis.

27 The ash from bonfires is a valuable source of potash. Scatter some round fruit trees (March if possible) to increase the yield.

28 In the organic vegetable garden, you feed the soil rather than give supplements to the plant. Organic manure rather than artificial fertilisers is necessary and good homemade liquid fertilisers can be made by soaking bags of soot, mature farmyard manure, comfrey or seaweed extracts in water. Leave to soak, drain off the liquid and give to your plants.

29 Gather plenty of oak leaves for the compost heap and also to mulch round plants which are particularly prone to slug and snail attacks.

30 Birch leaves make a valuable addition to a compost heap as they disinfect the soil, preventing fly diseases.

31 Banana skins baked in the oven and dug under the soil around rose beds add potassium-rich goodness for vigorous growth.

32 Beer is a drink that hollyhocks love; it's the yeast that works wonders.

33 Save dried tea and coffee bags. Open them up and sprinkle them on the lawn or garden for an instant fertiliser.

34 Bury old leather boots and shoes in the garden rather than chuck them in the dustbin. When the leather eventually rots down, it adds all manner of nutrients to the soil.

35   For an even better show of irises next year, sprinkle Epsom salts in crystal form round their rhizomes in summer.

36   Tomato plants which look pale and anaemic with yellow leaves could be short of magnesium and need a spray or drink of Epsom salts – 2 ozs (57g) per gallon (4.5l) of tepid water.

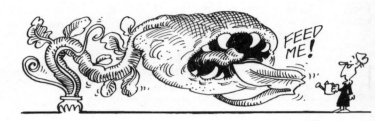

37   Tea leaves make the perfect mulch for camellias.

38   Dull and droopy ferns may be crying out for food. Invest in a small bottle of castor oil; add it to the roots and watch them take on a new lease of life. A piece of raw beef worked well down into the soil – taking care not to damage the roots – is a less conventional fertiliser.

39   To make daffodils an even brighter yellow, mix dry mustard with fertiliser when you plant the bulbs.

40   Rainwater, the cheapest and most easily available plant tonic around, contains carbolic acid and nitrates which act as a soil fertiliser.

41   To get the best from farmyard manure, shake the heap (with a fork), watering it to keep it moist and turn it over at regular intervals, turning the outside edges into the centre for even rotting throughout. The bacterial properties will heat it up and break it down to a crumbly mixture – eventually. Don't ever put strong farmyard manure straight on to the soil and even in a fully rotted state, dig it deep down.

42 Poultry (and pigeon) droppings are a highly concentrated form of animal manure and must be applied sparingly. They are best used in dried form to cut down the risk of scorching.

43 Sheep manure is a rich source of nutrients, and just ahead of horse manure in order of merit as plant food. Cow and pig manures are the also rans. They haven't a great deal to offer and, being sloppy, are too wet for all but sandy soils.

44 Stable and other animal manures are best protected from rain and air. Mix them with a little soil as you turn the growing pile over, and cover with another 6 inches (15cm) of soil to mature until ready for use.

Seeds

45 Resist the temptation to dig and make a seed bed in one go. For best results, dig during a dry spell in late autumn or early winter and sow in the spring. The winter frosts will turn the rough surface into a crumbly workable texture, which you can firm off (with feet) and lightly rake over.

46 Thinnings should be completely removed. Replant them else-where if needed, or bury them well into the compost heap. The unwanted thinned plants give off a strong odour as they die, attracting pests to the remaining, less pungent plants.

47　A good trick for sowing tiny seeds more thinly on soil, is to mix a small amount with some sand in a sugar shaker or a plastic yoghurt-pot with holes in the bottom.

48　For larger seeds, where a hole is drilled but the seed is difficult to handle, drop them through a small plastic funnel. Cut off the top section from a plastic washing up bottle and use as a makeshift funnel, or use a folded piece of paper. Another method is to put the seeds in a saucer of water and, using a small piece of broken glass, fish the seeds out one by one, using the tip of the glass. Once transferred like this, the seed is easily dislodged by gently tapping the glass against a hole.

49　Never throw away cellophane. This can be tied loosely round a favourite flowering plant in the garden to collect seeds.

50　When thinning seedlings it helps if (a) they have been sown as thinly as possible in the first place, and (b) when seedlings are large enough to handle, instead of pulling them up, simply cut them off just above ground level.

51　To take seeds from clematis, make a funnel-shaped cellophane collar secured with sellotape when the feathery seeds have turned a silver colour. Sow them in sandy compost in March and keep them in a cold frame in the dark. You will need great faith and patience, plus the usual element of luck, as germination can take up to a year.

52　Seeds with a hard outer coating, such as sweet peas, need a little help to germinate. First soak them in warm water for 24 hours (in a saucer on top of an Aga or in a thermos flask) to soften them up. The alternative is to make a nick in the seed with a sharp knife to help the fleshy part push through.

53　With tiny seeds which are difficult to treat by hand, line a jar with the roughest emery paper you can find and shake them round inside.

54   Keep an old plastic Jiffy lemon juice container in the greenhouse for watering tender young seedlings drop by drop without damaging the roots.

55   Don't buy special seed trays. Cardboard egg boxes make excellent peat containers for young seedlings, one seedling per compartment. The box can go straight into the ground when planting out, as the cardboard will disintegrate.

56   A used, squeezed-out tea bag makes the ideal nursery for a single seed starting out in life. Pop the seed inside the tea bag and put 2 or 3 of these into a small pot of compost. Perfect drainage, extra nourishment and easy to plant out without damaging the young roots.

57   Never throw away an old broom handle. It's the perfect implement for making a shallow seed trench. Lay the handle along the soil and press it down firmly by walking along it. The imprint leaves a straight 1 inch (2.5cm) deep trench.

58   Probably the best place for keeping leftover seeds is in a cool pantry in a labelled, airtight tin container. They will rapidly deteriorate in warm kitchens and sunny garden sheds. They can also be kept in the salad compartment of the fridge for up to 3 months. It really is important to take time to label everything, to prevent bulbs going into stews and seeds being sprinkled on salads etc. It does happen.

59 When sowing seeds in hot weather, germination can be severely hampered by over-dry soil. For best results, make a drill where the seeds will go and carefully fill this up with water, using a watering can with a fine spout. Let the water soak in, add the seed, firm in gently, then cover with dry soil which acts as a mulch preventing the evaporation of the water.

See also 69.

Cuttings

60 You sometimes acquire cuttings without the means to pot them straight away. Pop them immediately into a clear plastic bag and place them, labelled, in the salad drawer of the fridge. They'll be none the worse for a few days until you can offer them a more permanent home.

61 Once trimmed, it can be difficult to remember which way round cuttings should be inserted in the soil. Make a point of always cutting straight across the top (the farthest bit from the stem) and diagonally at the bottom.

62 Press soil or compost round cuttings fairly firmly; if loose they won't root. If cuttings can be easily pulled from the potting compost, it indicates that they are not planted firmly enough.

See also 5, 66.

Spring and Summer

63 Take photographs throughout spring and summer to show where improvements could be made, extra shrubs and plants added, others thinned out or transplanted. Use graph paper to plan a bedding scheme illustrating planting distances, colour schemes etc.

64 Many bargains in herbaceous plants are to be found in mail order catalogues. If the roots are dry on arrival, soak them in a bucket of water for 24 hours, but if any are clearly damaged, tell the nursery at once so that they can replace them. Your legal rights when buying goods by mail order are the same as those when buying from a shop; ie they must be as described, fit for the purpose, and of merchantable quality.

65 Many plants which settle in and appear to be thriving in the greenhouse collapse when insufficient attention is paid to 'hardening off'. It's essential to introduce more air slowly – over a 3 to 4 week period, preferably up to the middle of May.

66 In March, you can take geranium cuttings from overwintered plants. Cut off 3 inch (7.5cm) long shoot tips immediately below a leaf joint or node. Strip all but the topmost pair of leaves and insert these cuttings up to half their depth in small pots of compost. Water and place in a reasonably warm, well lit spot – a window ledge is ideal – until they root. Once established, they can be transplanted to bigger pots to allow them to expand before hardening off and planting out in summer.

67 If you have any old rubber tyres, use them to protect young spring vegetables and plants from lingering winter frosts. Plant them inside the tyre and cover with a sheet of polythene. They can be thinned out and replanted later in warmer weather.

68 You can alter the colour of hydrangeas without buying new plants by sprinkling lime around the plant for pink, and adding a tablet of aluminium sulphate to the watering can for blue.

69 Increase your yield of sweet peas by placing crushed eggshells under the seeds when planting.

70 Although often on sale in shops from early April, most summer bedding plants shouldn't be planted out until all danger of frost is past, which, as any Scot will tell you, is not until May is safely ended. Unless bought when you are ready to plant them, early plants will become root bound or straggly in their containers, whatever measures you take to protect them.

71 'Pinch out' the tops of flowers and plants which tend to grow long and spindly. Use thumb and forefinger to remove the growing shoot tips and encourage bushiness in plants such as wallflowers and coleus. Side shoots will quickly appear, giving the plant a healthier, more attractive shape.

72 Never water plants in a lower temperature than the one they're already in. Plants reared under glass need tepid water to avoid causing damage to the roots by cooling them down.

73 The rule for planting lilies is face in the sun, feet in the shade. An ideal habitat is in between shrubs. However, if overcrowding becomes a problem, after 3 years you can lift them as soon as a week after flowering, and find them a fresh bed.

74 Where plants are purchased without soil attached to the roots and there is a delay in replanting, store in a cool place and always plant to the same level as the soil mark on the stems.

Autumn and Winter

75 Herbaceous plants running amok will benefit from being lifted and divided into smaller clumps. When a plant is too big to break up by hand, the recommended method of separating it is with a couple of garden forks pushed back to back in the centre and forced apart, but you can use a sharp knife. If the new clumps have a good number of buds and fresh young roots, they will quickly re-establish themselves.

76 If you have to transplant out of season when the ground is too cold, pour hot water into the hole to heat it sufficiently – it won't harm the roots.

77 Frequent collecting and burning of dead leaves and twigs helps to stop the spread of diseases and pest infestation. By removing dead shoots, flowers and seed pods, you can encourage the plant to produce fresh shoots and flowers, extending the growing period.

78 Protect and store gladioli over winter by lifting after flowering and placing in a damp-free ventilated place to dry out completely. Removing the soil from the root, cut back the tops and rinse the corms in an appropriate fungicide solution to prevent any spread of disease. Label and store them where frost can't harm them.

79 In very cold winters, protect delicate plants with a blanket of straw, leaves or bracken. Re-usable gardener's netting secured with twigs does the job of holding the cover in place from the end of autumn until spring.

80 After flowering, dahlias should be dug up and cut back until the top growth is about 6 inches (15cm). Leave the tubers upturned in a cool place to drain moisture from the stems. Remove the soil and trim off any damaged sections before planting the tubers right way up in dry peat or sand, protected from damp or frost during the winter.

81 When geraniums finish flowering in autumn, plant in compost in pots in a well lit, ventilated, not too warm spot. Water very occasionally to stop them drying out until you are ready to plant them out again.

82 Chrysanthemums, at the end of the season's flowering, need a head trim to 6 inches (15cm) from the root. Place the rootstocks in compost, water very occasionally in a frost-free dry place, and label for easy replanting next year.

83 Oddly enough, you can protect outdoor plants from impending frost by spraying them with cold water in the evening. As it evaporates, the water generates sufficient heat to prevent frost damage.

84 Emergency treatment for frozen plants in a greenhouse calls for a gentle thaw of the plants by pouring on cold water in the dark; they'll die if watered in light.

Outdoor Bulbs

85 To get best value from garden bulbs they should be divided, in order to multiply, every other year. Many varieties will double in number each time this procedure is carried out.

86 The best time to dig up, divide and replant spring bulbs is while they are well beyond flowering but still 'in the green' ie in June or early July before the stems have withered and died back. Water well both before lifting (digging deep enough to clear the roots) and afterwards after replanting to minimise the shock, keeping the bulbs out of the ground for the shortest possible time in between.

87 To remove bulbs to another site when they can't be immediately transplanted, dig them up carefully with plenty of root attached, but keep them in moist peat with the leaves free and water in well as soon as you can replant them.

88 If it is impractical to keep bulbs moist, whether in the ground or in peat bags, the alternative is to let them dry out in a well ventilated place – flat on newspapers or hung up in bunches – and restart them between August and October.

89 Best sites for crocuses are round tree bases or other shady spots below hedges and shrubs. For an attractive display mix with snowdrops and lily-of-the-valley.

90 Tulips need to be in a sunny spot with good drainage. Ideally you should plant them in October or November, but you can get away with later planting up to Christmas.

91 A nightmare for tulip lovers is an outbreak of 'tulip fire'. This distorts and stunts the flowers which develop yellowish streaky spots on their foliage. Prevent this calamity by religiously collecting up tulip petals or snapping off spent flowers, cutting off and destroying yellow leaves.

92 Tulips tend to do well for cat owners, as mice consider tulips a great delicacy, nibbling off their tops. If you can't keep a watch cat, traps and anti-rodent powders and potions are the only answer if bald patches start to get you down.

93 Tulip bulbs can be attacked below ground level by black slugs. A deadly slug food called Nobble, if used regularly until the leaves emerge from the soil, will confine its killer instinct to the slugs, but won't harm birds or other animals.

94 Manure is too strong for tulips if placed near them during the growing process. Use well draining compost to feed the bulbs before they flower and only add manure to enrich the soil and improve moisture retention once the bulbs have been lifted.

95 Some types of tulips, the large Darwin Hybrids such as Apeldoorn, will keep growing vigorously for up to 5 years without lifting, providing the soil is of good quality, well drained and the bulbs are planted quite deeply. A good tip is to water them after they've flowered using Phostrogen foliar feed to nourish the bulbs in preparation for another healthy burst the following season.

See also 2, 39, 116, 117.

Watering

96 Always fit a rose on a watering can to avoid washing away valuable compost and exposing the roots once plants are in place.

97 When hosepipe bans are in operation, even the bathwater will do a good job of keeping plants alive – a mild soapy solution is one of the recommended treatments for pest control. A heavy watering now and again does far more good to vegetables in particular than dribs and drabs applied frequently.

98 Where large areas are to be well watered with an ordinary hose stick a flower pot or a tin can, with the top and bottom removed, well into the soil and direct the hose end in this to soak the earth without splashing it everywhere.

See also 11, 12, 14, 72, 119.

Butterflies

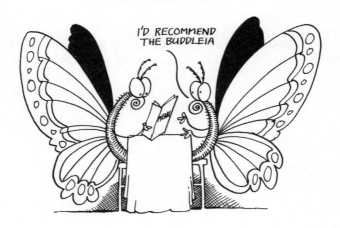

99 Don't waste money on 'cons' such as special plants and 'caterpillar food' for butterfly gardening. Nettlebeds are particularly good hostelries for butterflies, provided they are in an undisturbed sunny spot. The white Davidii species of buddleia is also popular, but they actually prefer the mauve flowering variety which grows wild on derelict sites. Other old-fashioned plants to their liking are michaelmas daisies, pussy willows, scented wallflowers, honesty and forget-me-not.

See also 186

Climbers and Creepers

100 Stuck with an ugly, broken down fence, rusty tin roof or similar eye-sore? Plant a Russian vine which has an abundance of creamy white flowers and an incredibly fast growth rate – up to 20 feet (6m) a year.

101 When your virginia creeper won't creep, it needs a friendly hand and small pieces of waterproof sticking plaster to tape its shoots to the wall until they get the hang of it themselves.

102 Plasticine or Blu-tack is handy stuff for training young trailing plants, ivy and so on, up a wall.

103 Many gardeners prefer ivy which has tiny pad-like suckers to secure itself rather than many climbers with roots which dig into loose brickwork and plaster. If the main stem of ivy is severed the plant will die and within a few weeks can be pulled from the wall. Contrary to popular belief, ivy does not make a house damp; in fact it protects the wall from the elements, making it drier.

See also 146, 270.

Ponds and Pools

104 Where there are young children (young pets and hedgehogs too) using a garden, make sure that a garden pond is covered with a sturdy safety net. Many parents prefer to turn ponds into sand pits or rock gardens until children are old enough to understand the dangers.

See also 273.

| 105 | Never strike a blow to break up ice where fish are underneath; the shock waves can damage, even kill them. Place a hot kettle on top of the ice to thaw it out, or fill a plastic bottle with hot water and leave it (with string attached to retrieve it later) on top of the surface. |

| 106 | Prevent garden pools from freezing over by placing a rubber ball on top. The gentle movement helps stop the ice forming. |

Health and Safety

| 107 | Back problems prevent or put an end to the gardener's more strenuous activities. It's a fact that the longer the handle on an implement, the greater the leverage, and consequently the less strain on the back. If you are more than 5ft 4in (1.6m) tall, an ordinary spade is unhealthily short. Make lighter work of digging and do your back a favour with a Spear and Jackson long-handled version of their Neverbend Spade (Model 1150 EP). |

| 108 | Veteran gardeners rub elder leaves into their joints after a day's gardening to prevent stiffness and rheumatic pain, and a handful of Epsom salts under the running water as you fill a hot bath at the end of the day also does wonders for tiredness and aching limbs. |

| 109 | Slip a plastic bag over the top of garden canes and stand them in a piece of drainpipe to help prevent the many eye injuries which result from careless storage when they're not in use. |

| 110 | Keep tetanus injections up to date and always wear protective gloves when pruning, not just to prevent scratches and cuts but because many plants can cause allergic rashes or blistering to sensitive skin. |

| 111 | A great many accidents, some fatal, occur each year in the garden and a good number are related to shocks from hedge trimmers, mowers and other power driven gadgets. It makes sense therefore to invest in a power breaker for safety's sake. The other sensible buy when strimming or shredding, is a pair of goggles. |

Lawns

| 112 | Exercise and tone your ankles while giving your lawn the best possible start in life! Better than lugging a heavy roller over a new seed bed and leaving uneven bumpy bits which it misses, is to 'heel' in the soil. Go slowly over each and every bit of the new lawn in really short steps with your weight over your heels to push out air pockets and soft patches. Rake and repeat. |

| 113 | For an evenly sown lawn divide the area equally into squares, allocating the same amount of seed for each. Divide each portion again by half, scattering the seeds in opposite directions per square. A final light raking over the whole lot should make sure that it's now evenly distributed. |

| 114 | There are two schools of thought about whether grass cuttings left on a lawn do more harm than good. Certainly they return goodness to the soil, retaining valuable moisture. Against this, the decomposing cuttings encourage earthworms to come up and munch on them and invariably encourage weeds which are more difficult and costly to remove. |

115   A quick and easy way to trim the sides of a lawn is by laying a plank flat along its edges and digging the straggly bits into line using the sharp edge of a spade.

116   Snowdrops, crocuses and daffodils scattered ad-lib across a lawn may look delightfully natural but they inhibit the cutting of the grass, which in turn causes it to deteriorate. You can still get the spring woodland look by growing them in drifts under trees.

117   Grassy banks can become slippery and dangerous as well as being difficult to keep in trim. Save time and make life easier by covering the area with ground cover plants combined with spring bulbs.

118   Small patches of grass which are difficult to mow and become bare with constant use, where they lead to garden sheds or in front of houses for example, could be covered with paving stones or gravel (with black polythene underneath to suffocate weeds) for easy maintenance and to make the area seem surprisingly more spacious. Compare the prices between DIY shops, garden centres and gravel suppliers (Yellow Pages) if ordering a large quantity.

119   Don't risk a fine during a hosepipe ban. Water shouldn't be given to lawns unless a long drought makes it necessary, as once begun it must be continued at least once a week for as long as the drought continues. Watering encourages weeds and clover rather than grass which seems to stand dry weather better than weeds. Brown, scorched and apparently dead grass recovers amazingly quickly after a shower or two of rain.

120 If a lawn becomes really overgrown, cut the length of the grass back in stages. The shock, if severely cut back, makes the grass less sturdy and it will need fertiliser to stimulate the growth.

121 On cold mornings, never walk on a lawn which is covered with frost. It will be brittle and easily damaged.

122 Earthworms are generally believed to do more harm than good to a lawn. Although their burrowings provide natural drainage, they make the surface muddy and soft, weakening the soil and wearing it out more quickly if walked on. Their casts encourage weeds which should be brushed off a lawn, never rolled or mown in. Get rid of them by watering the soil with an inexpensive solution of ½ oz (15g) of potassium permanganate per gallon (4.5l) of water.

Hedges

123 Boundary hedges backing on to grazing land should never contain yew as this is poisonous to animals. Inexpensive and suitable alternatives for the job include hawthorn, privet and beech, which can be protected by a wire-mesh outer fence until mature.

124 Young hedges grow leggy and bare unless well fed and properly pruned in their formative years. Reduce the top level considerably to encourage it to grow sideways and trim off the straggly side-shoots to gradually form an even edge over 2 or 3 years. This way further side shoots are encouraged to fill the gaps.

`125` For a useful guideline when hedge trimming, stretch a length of twine along the top of 2 posts placed at either end, at the required level. Stick bamboo canes at intervals as vertical indicators for the side trim.

`126` Save time and energy when hedge trimming by putting down a collecting sheet and then cutting the hedge from the base upwards. This saves you from constantly having to stop and remove trimmings that fall on an uncut bit underneath. Make sure your shears are sharp or they will leave jagged tears in branches which makes it easier for disease and rot to set in.

`127` If you can't decide between a fence which may be too stark in front of a house or a hedge which dies back in winter and may not be robust enough to dissuade dogs, cats and newsboys from climbing through, you could try a 'fedge'. After putting up a simple fence, train colourful forsythia, berberis or honeysuckle plants round the supports. For a more dense cover in green and cream, try variegated ivy.

`128` Don't waste money on a mechanical hedge trimmer, or even shears, for a laurel hedge, as the leaves will turn brown. Painstaking trimming of individual branches with secateurs will pay dividends.

Roses

<hr>

129   When roses have grown too old or neglected beyond redemption and replacements are necessary, the soil where they've been is most likely to be 'rose sick'. Despite well intentioned efforts to add extra nourishment to the ground, the new bushes are unlikely to do well. Put a different type of plant where the old roses have been and find another bed for the new arrivals.

130   As a rule of thumb, roses with large or cluster flowers should be planted 18–24 inches (45–60cm) apart so as not to restrict their growth. More vigorous varieties may well need more and it's best to take advice from the supplier to give them the best start.

131   Mail ordered roses should ideally have 3 or 4 strong canes of at least pencil thickness on a healthy specimen. The bark should be firm and unwrinkled and the plant must have plenty of fibrous roots with a thumb's thickness or more from the root to the point where the shoots start growing.

132   November is the best month for planting roses. Always drive the supporting stake into the ground before placing the root ball in the hole to avoid damaging it. Planting deeper than the soil mark on the stem will only encourage suckers, so it's important to check that the level is right. Tie quite loosely to the supporting stake for the first couple of weeks until the rose settles itself comfortably into its new bed.

133   Pruning roses is all important for their development, but disease can spread through dirty secateurs. Keep them clean and sharp, especially to prevent jagged edges which are particularly vulnerable. Cutting ¼ inch (6mm) from an outward facing bud (with the cut slanting down away from the bud) will encourage a vigorous growth.

<hr>

134 Newly planted roses (with the exception of climbers which should be left for a year) can be pruned even more drastically than older, established bushes to build a strong foundation for new shoots to start. It may seem savage, but 2–3 inches (5–7.5cm) long is recommended by nursery men.

135 'Never let a friend prune your roses' my green-fingered Scots mother used to say. The theory, borne out by the previous tip, is that he or she would be too gentle, afraid of hurting the plant and upsetting you by drastic cutting. For the kindly sorts, there is plenty of evidence to suggest that whereas severe pruning gives vigorous growth, a lighter trim rewards the tender with more flowers.

136 An idea popular in France and a blessing for those who like attractive, easily kept gardens, is to designate an area for growing roses, and prepare the ground as you normally would for a good, well fertilised bed. Then place black PVC liner to cover the entire area, but making slits where you want the rose bushes to grow. Place them into the ground up to the soil mark, and after watering and firming in, cover the polythene with gravel. Extra moisture can be added at the stem when necessary.

137 Pruning diagrams in books don't have a fraction of the teaching power of seeing an expert perform the task 'live'. There are free demonstrations throughout the country given by gardening societies and specialist nurseries such as:

The Royal National Rose Society   Mattocks Rose Nursery
Chiswell Green   Nuneham Courtney
St Albans   Oxfordshire OX9 9PY
Hertfordshire AL2 3NR   Tel: 086 738265
Tel: 0727 50461

Write enclosing SAE to request 'What's On' and when.

138 An old wives' trick for a healthy rose tree is to take a square of grass and place it, face downwards, to cover the bottom of the newly dug hole. Spread the roots on top and continue to fill up as usual.

139 The rose revived: jaded roses will often respond to a tonic made from soot collected from a wood-burning chimney. Place the soot in a container and pour boiling water over it. Allow the liquid to settle and cool before applying it daily to the roses. Dramatic changes in colour and vigour have been reported, so it's worth a try on other sickly species.

140 Although a lump of fat or dripping bedded below it is a valuable if unconventional boost for roses, it's not particularly practical where dogs, cats or even foxes can dig it up. Where they can't it works wonders. Alternatively, 1 oz (25g) of Epsom salts in a gallon (4.5l) of water every few weeks is a cheap and efficacious tonic for rose bushes.

141 Grow parsley near roses; one of the prettier feathery varieties won't look out of place in a flower bed, and will enhance the scent of the rose. Parsley also encourages bees and repels greenfly.

142 To make rosewater, collect 1 lb (450g) of the freshest petals of heavily scented roses, eg Ena Harkness, and fill an old kettle with water. Drop in the petals and stand the kettle on a gentle heat. Attach one length of a rubber hose to the kettle spout, the other to a jar or bottle. When steam starts to rise, rest the middle section of the tube in iced water to cool it and so drip the concentrated rose water into the container until nearly all the water from the kettle evaporates. Seal the bottle tightly.

143   Always collect petals when the early morning dew has dried off completely to avoid mildew. No need to leave blooms bald; just take a couple at a time and separate and dry the petals carefully, building up a stock of pot pourri gradually over the summer.

144   Home-made pot pourri is much cheaper and nicer than shop bought varieties. It is absolutely essential that only unblemished petals at the peak of their freshness, and not just past it, are used to ensure a strong scent. This easy recipe requires:

3 parts highly scented rose petals (dried in an airy room away from sunlight)
1 part mix of dried thyme and dried rosemary
The dried, powdered skin of a 'lightly' peeled orange or lemon (low on pith, high on zest)
A few bay leaves
½ oz (15g) of crushed cloves
1 teaspoon Allspice.

Mix all the ingredients well in a suitable pot pourri bowl.

145   Floral air freshener. A teaspoon or two of rosewater mixed with powdered cloves soaked up in cotton wool and placed in a warm spot – or in the airing cupboard to scent the linen – makes a wonderful freshener. In the old days this delicious scent was placed on a hot pan and left inside a bed to perfume and air sheets.

146   When choosing a rose for wallcover, select a climber rather than a rambler which is more prone to mildew. Fix horizontal wires, about 18 inches (45cm) apart, and secured with 'vine eyes' to the brickwork, keeping the wire about 3 in (7.5cm) out from the wall. Always train the shoots horizontally rather than allowing them to grow straight up. This encourages flowering shoots to grow low, along their length and not just at the tips.

See also 31, 328, 353.

The Kitchen Garden

Getting Started

147 If the object of growing your own vegetables is to save money, avoid the types which are generally plentiful and therefore cheaper in shops – carrots, onions, cabbages etc – cultivate purple sprouting broccoli, green peppers etc. If you are growing for goodness and flavour however, try early carrots, spinach and salad vegetables including less common varieties of tomatoes and sweetcorn which rapidly deteriorate in quality once dispatched to the shops.

148 Bewildered by choice, novice vegetable growers will find that runner beans, courgettes, marrows, potatoes and spinach are very easy to grow. Shallots, lettuce, calabrese and beetroot are close runners up in the trouble free stakes.

149 When funds won't stretch to a greenhouse, see the adverts for polythene tunnels (in gardening magazines, the Sunday newspaper classified ads etc). Inexpensive and easy to erect, no foundations are necessary, so they are easily transported to another site if required.

150 Rotating groups of vegetables around the kitchen garden each year is recommended to control the build up of diseases which favour one botanical variety more than another. The main groups are legumes (peas and beans), brassicas (broccoli, brussels sprouts, cabbages, cauliflower, turnip, swede, kale and chinese cabbage), the onion family (which includes garlic and shallots) and potatoes and tomatoes.

151 Job lots of plain net curtains from jumble sales, dyed wood green and sewn together, can be turned into netting for a vegetable patch.

152 Plastic bottles over the tops of stick/twigs/bamboo canes supporting netting will protect it from snagging or tearing.

153 You can double the choice on the family menu by growing two-faced vegetables such as courgettes – which if left to grow on become marrows – and mangetout, the sugar pea, where the whole pod is eaten in its early picking state, but develops into a common or garden variety for shelling when allowed to mature.

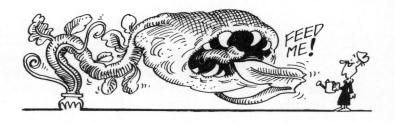

FEED ME!

154 Pick the tops from very young nettles and cook for a delicious vegetable not unlike spinach.

155 Lettuces, radishes and cabbages are among the vegetables which won't store well. Sow them in a short row every few weeks; otherwise you'll have a glut. You might be able to arrange a 'swap' system with another gardener.

156 Longer does not necessarily mean bigger and better. When growing vegetables the skill is in learning when they are at their peak in flavour and freshness and picking them at once. Cucumbers, peas, beans and marrows, for example, must be picked regularly. Left on the plant when they reach maturity, they can close down the production line completely.

157 To bring crop rotation down to its simplest form, divide vegetables into 2 categories; those which grow above the ground one season and those which grow below it the next.

158 American fruit growers store their apples in between layers of maple leaves. Works well for preserving root vegetables too.

159 Unless peas, beans, tomatoes, cucumbers, marrows and courgettes are heavily watered when they start to flower, the yield will be less. So in the absence of heavy rain at this crucial time, it's important to water by hand.

160 To get the maximum use from a small vegetable plot, intercrop radishes, spring onions, small lettuces etc in between taller-growing brussels sprouts and sweetcorn.

161 Organic vegetables are expensive in the shops, but not many people have the space for growing their own. Perhaps an elderly person in your area with room to spare for a vegetable plot would agree to your doing the work and sharing the produce.

Get more mileage from artichokes. You can increase the size of the head if, once the stalk is fully developed, you make 2 incisions in it just below the head, and insert 2 matchsticks crossing each other.

See also 1, 218, 222.

Brassicas (Cabbages, Sprouts and Cauliflowers)

 If cabbage and cauliflower heads have a tendency to split open, nip this practice in the bud by making an incision in the stalk on one side beneath the head and insert a small wood chipping in the cut.

 If cabbages or sprouts have mildew, spray them with water heavily laced with methylated spirits.

 Get a second crop of cabbages from a single stalk. Spring and summer varieties lend themselves well to this thrifty trick. Leave the stalk in the ground after cutting off the cabbage head. You then cut a ¼ inch (6mm) deep cross with a sharp knife on top of the stalk. Given plenty of moisture and good-ness in the soil, you should get as many as half a dozen new buds growing below the cross which will be fully grown for picking by the end of the summer.

166   Cabbages are prone to the disease clubroot which is especially difficult to control, particularly in acid soil. To protect the young plants, you should bury sticks of rhubarb alongside as you bed them in.

167   To keep a cauliflower white, (as opposed to yellow in sunlight or blackened with frost) break a few of its leaves off and make a protective cap for its head.

Fruit

168   An overgrown blackberry bush has at least one thing in its favour – you can propagate it easily. Bury its strongest shoot tips 4 inches (10cm) deep into the ground in July and August, peg them down with pebbles, stones or an old-fashioned clothes peg, cover them with compost, firm and water them in. The next spring your new plants should have established a good root, ready for trimming and transplanting.

169   To force rhubarb, lift a root or two in February and replant it in a large pot or box in the greenhouse. Cover it with black polythene or an upturned dustbin to exclude the light. Given sufficient warmth, shoots will put in an appearance quite quickly.

170   Rhubarb which is starting to look spindly and anaemic needs a complete overhaul in autumn when the leaves have died down. Lift the whole plant out of the ground and use a sharp edged spade to divide the crown into 2 or even 3 sections. Providing each has a substantial root and bud they can be replanted 5–6 feet (1.5m) apart in new, well fertilised territory. Repeat this process after about 5 years and in the meantime keep the clumps well fed and watered.

171 Just as you can train rose bushes into trees, so you can 'leg it' with gooseberries for easy picking and to leave ground space free for other things. In the autumn, take 18–24 inch (45–60cm) young wood cuttings, removing all but the 3 or 4 top buds. Make a thin trench in the soil and plant the cuttings a good half way up their length, firming and watering them in. By the following autumn, they should have a foot (30cm) long 'leg' and can then be transplanted to a permanent site.

172 Make healthy blackcurrant jam and juice with the variety known as 'Baldwin', found to have the highest vitamin C content.

173 To get maximum value for your money and greatest benefit to the budding fruit, apply fertilisers to apple and pear trees no later than late February or the beginning of March.

174 Most apple trees need another, blossoming in unison, nearby for pollination, but you can buy just one 'family tree' which has 3 varieties grafted on to a standard single stem. Ask at your local nursery.

175 Dead branches on fruit trees should be sawn off cleanly and close to the trunk in early May. Dress the cuts at once with a wood sealant from garden centres.

176 If you have a greenhouse, growing melons isn't too difficult and, of course, they are very pricey in the shops. Save string bags from greengrocers and old net curtains as useful props for supporting the weighty fruit. Only permit 3 or 4 fruits to develop per plant; pick off the others as soon as they start to swell.

177 Instead of the conventional straw blanket under strawberry plants, try plastic sheeting to keep the fruit clean while controlling weeds and retaining warmth and moisture around the beds.

178   Moth balls, it would appear, are of endless use to the gardener. One of their most famous tricks is to stop leaf curl on peach trees, but for easy hanging buy the Mothax rings and suspend them from the branches.

179   When planting a peach tree, sink a pipe down with it (ideally 2 inches (5cm) in diameter and 2 feet (60cm) down) allowing the top to just show above the surface for easy watering. This encourages the tree roots to go well down and keeps a good reserve of moisture.

See also 27, 158.

Herbs

180   Apart from drying herbs on a baking tray in a barely warm oven, you can preserve a supply by freezing. Parsley, for example, when picked, washed and popped into a plastic bag, will scrunch up in its frozen state allowing you to take out just the amount of readily broken pieces required for soups etc.

181   Mint runs riot and needs to be contained in a herb garden. An old washing up bowl with a couple of drainage holes added and sunk in the ground will do. Lift the mint up and divide into smaller clumps when it outgrows the tub.

182 Parsley can be difficult to grow from seed unless you pour boiling water on it before sowing, to speed the germination process.

183 Marigolds may seem a little out of place in a kitchen garden, but their culinary uses are well known to thrifty cooks who use their petals to colour food instead of wildly expensive saffron. Their flavour is a light, delicate one and they are easy to dry and keep if placed in a cool, dark place in thin layers to preserve their rich colour.

See also 244.

184 Ash from a bonfire can kill mint, so place it on roots if a mint clump has to be dug up and removed, but never as a mulch if you want mint to thrive.

185 To stop herb plants growing tall and spindly, pinch out the tops for nice bushy plants. Dry their seed heads by placing them in a brown paper bag and hanging them in a dry, warm place – above an Aga or in an airing cupboard is ideal.

186 Lavender plants, pretty to look at and deliciously scented will provide much appreciated sweet smelling sachets for Xmas presents (keeping moths at bay in drawers and wardrobes). As an added bonus, in their growing state they encourage butterflies to settle in the garden.

See also 4, 206, 210, 211, 212.

Legumes (Peas and Beans)

187 Get French beans off to a good start by sowing them indoors. Arrange the seeds on damp newspaper, leaving them overnight to absorb moisture and plump out a little before sowing them in quality potting compost. Make sure they're thoroughly hardened off and well watered before transferring outdoors.

188 Pinch out the top of broad beans when the pods start to come; you'll now have an extra-palatable vegetable when lightly boiled.

189 Cross the supporting canes for runner beans no more than half way up their height from ground level. The beans will then hang outwards for quick and easy picking.

190 Watering the leaves of runner beans (and sweet peas) as well as the soil during very dry weather is essential for a bumper crop.

See also 235, 314.

Onions, Garlic and Leeks

191 Some onions store better than others and when buying seed it's best to check. Onions which sprout after picking and storing lose much of their goodness. Singeing the roots of each onion with a red hot poker will prevent this. It also improves their chances of survival in good condition if, after picking, you take care not to bend the leaves as they die back naturally in warm sun for several days to dry them out. Alternatively leave them flat in a well ventilated, cool place and take care not to bruise them when handling and plaiting them – or packing them in old nylon stockings or tights.

192   Tip from the French who know their onions – and garlic, best. The timing is all important when planting garlic. Plant cloves in the second week of March to get one big round clove instead of several small ones. Garlic cloves planted between October and February will produce heads of several smaller ones.

193   It's said by Mediterranean gardeners, who cultivate vast amounts of it, that if you bruise garlic cloves gently by crushing them before planting it will improve the flavour. They sow it along with olive stones for best results.

194   Maggots are somewhat partial to leeks. Prize leek growers prop eggshells on small sticks between the plants to encourage butterflies to lay their eggs there instead of on the leeks. Another favourite ploy is provided by tomatoes. Planted next to leeks, butterflies are repelled by the smell.

See also 2.

Potatoes

195   Potatoes take up so much space in the small vegetable garden and can often be bought more cheaply in the shops, unless you get the perfect spud you like for cooking. Grow Desirée for best boilers, Cara for perfect jacket potatoes and Scottish Kerr's Pink for unbeatable chips.

196 Double your money, and potato crop too, by cutting each seed potato in two. Provided that each half has healthy shoots, it should develop into a full plant.

197 Potatoes will store best in hessian or stout brown paper bags in a cool, dark, frost-free place.

Root Crops

198 To keep celeriac and parsnip, leave them in the ground at the end of their growing season but protect them with a blanket of straw to keep the ground pliable for lifting when the ground is frosty.

199 Collect boxes of sand in which to bed layers of turnips, swedes, carrots and beetroot. Fine ash or dry peat can be substituted for the sand.

200 Where salsify is growing crooked and forked, the problem could lie in too shallow planting. Straight, sturdy plants need a bed of deep dug, well nourished soil.

See also 158.

Good
– and Bad –
Companions

201 Ash trees, although they make wonderful firewood, take a huge share of goodness from the soil whilst growing which could explain why anything planted within yards of them never seems to thrive without lashings of extra nutrition.

202 Fuschias love green bracken chopped up and laid underneath the roots when planting, or to cover them in cold weather.

203 Nettles do a good job in stimulating the growth of neighbouring plants. They also attract several species of butterfly.

204 Never plant gladioli near a vegetable patch as they'll have an ill effect on peas and beans and fatal consequences for strawberries.

205 Foxgloves keep disease at bay, both when planted near vegetables and herbs or flowers in the garden. Where foxgloves would spoil your planting scheme, it's still worth growing them in a clump in an odd corner as a medicinal compound for your plants. Foxglove tea – made by pouring boiling water on the leaves and flowers and leaving them to soak overnight – is invaluable as a tonic at watering times.

206 To give an extra strong flavour to mint, plant camomile next to it. Apart from having soothing, health-giving properties for humans when camomile leaves are made into a herbal tea, if planted next to tired, ailing plants in a flower or vegetable garden it will speed their recovery and produce more vigorous specimens of cabbages and onions in particular.

207 Onions and garlic get on as well with carrots in a vegetable garden as they do in a stew, but if placed near turnips, peas, beans and leeks, they won't do them any good. Everybody needs good neighbours they say, and time spent planning a vegetable patch to place plants where they are happiest, is well spent.

208 Sow plenty of turnip seeds where a vegetable plot is plagued by couch grass, and it should kill it off nicely. Couch rarely grows thickly round tomatoes or near lupins in a flower bed so presumably they have the same magical properties for tackling this persistent weed.

209 Never plant cabbages near your strawberries. They will be sure to kill them off.

210 Discourage cabbage moths by planting mint, thyme or dill near cabbage and broccoli.

211 Fennel and dill don't get along, so place them well apart in a herb garden.

212 Sage, mint, rosemary and thyme, versatile garden herbs in their own right, will keep cabbages pest and disease free if planted in close vicinity.

213 Radishes make the perfect neighbours for cabbages, stopping the ravages of maggots (and discouraging carrot fly to boot!).

214 Plant onions and carrots together to ward off onion fly.

215 Horseradish is the best companion for potatoes – beetles hate it.

See also 141, 166, 193, 244, 248, 333–338.

Weeding

216   Keep down weeds around herbaceous border plants the easy way by raking in the autumn leaves round them. Rotted down, they add valuable nutrients to the soil.

217   Kill unwanted grass in between paving stones by buying table salt in bulk, adding it to boiling water and pouring it over the grass.

218   To prevent weeds germinating and to keep in moisture on resting vegetable patches, make useful mulches from old carpet anchored with stones, heavy black polythene (such as dustbin liners) or even thick layers of newspaper or cardboard. Make sure they overlap and weigh them down firmly at the edges.

219   Constant hoeing is the best method of keeping weeds at bay in a herbaceous border as it's essential to stop annual weeds from seeding. Deep rooted perennials, eg dandelions and docks,

should be severed as far down in the ground as possible with a long-bladed knife.

220 For monster roots, such as elder, more drastic measures may be called for. Make incisions, or drill a hole and fill it with dry weedkiller/sodium chlorate and seal with melted candle wax to prevent leaking until the root rots away. Once the ground is weed free, 2 inches (5cm) of mulch will help keep them down.

221 To cut down weeding time, avoid using grass cuttings as a mulch when the grass is seeding.

222 Placing vegetables such as lettuces equal distances apart in all directions rather than in rows, will encourage uniform ground cover, depriving weeds of essential light supplies. Narrow leaved varieties (onions etc) will need extra hand weeding until they're established, when they can be mulched.

223 Hoe weeds in dry, sunny conditions, chopping them off before they can flower and seed. Hoeing in moist conditions is in-advisable. You may merely divide and transplant the weeds.

224 To get the best results from a weedkiller the weather must be fairly warm, so if you delay fertilising your grass until the April sun improves the conditions for both weeding and feeding, you can get best value for money and save time with a combined solution, eg Toplawn.

 March is a good time to spot the fresh young leaves of ground elder. If they are entwined around other roots of neighbouring plants that you want to keep, use the lifting process usefully to divide and replant them. Never put dug elder on a compost heap; burn it or bin it.

Creatures

226 If you scatter mustard powder round blooms it stops the ravages of worms.

227 A large nail stuck in the ground next to tomato plants keeps cutworms away.

228 Half fill shallow plastic pots or lay a jam jar on its side with beer or wine to trap slugs. It's kinder to hedgehogs too who may become tipsy, but won't be killed by lethal slug pellets.

229 Slugs seem to be particularly addicted to certain plants, such as hostas. If all else fails, plant them in raised containers—slugs don't jump.

230 A soot and wood ash mix is a total turn-off to slugs who, on the other hand, are much drawn to bran scattered round a crop. After eating it they die off quickly.

231 Make a slug conservatory. Keep the empty halves of squeezed oranges and put them face down where seedlings have been introduced to the garden. The slugs will collect underneath for childishly easy removal next day.

232 Horsehair wound round fruit trees will stop slugs and snails from climbing up trunks. If horsehair is difficult to get, try petroleum jelly.

233 Lucky the person who finds toads in their garden. They thrive on slugs and other destructive beasties.

234 Leave a bed of bran with cabbage leaves for covers and snails will obligingly check in overnight ready for an early morning collection.

235 Hedgehogs are well worth encouraging because of their amazing appetite for slugs and snails. To keep them in your garden, supply extra rations. Tinned cat and dog food and plain water are best. Milk, unless greatly watered down, and bread are not good for them.

236 If woodlice are eating away at your clematis buds, check whether the cane support is hollow. If it is, plug it—that's where the woodlice spend their days.

237   Squirrels and rabbits don't find mothballs much to their taste, so scatter a few round tomato plants and other edibles.

238   Rabbits, despite their cute powder puff tails, don't like talcum powder and sprinkling some around their favourite plants will send them hopping.

239   Mothballs can be an excellent deterrent. When moles play havoc with your lawn, try putting a handful of mothballs – or coffee grounds – in their runs. Crush a few mothballs around flower beds and dogs and cats will do a U-turn at the first whiff.

240   Dried orange or lemon peel, crumbled and scattered round bedding plants, will deter cats who like to use them as sunbeds. So will a bicycle tyre – they think it's a snake.

241   Newly sown ground seems to have a particular appeal to cats looking for a good scratch, as well as birds in search of a quick snack. Twigs stuck in the ground will stop cats, and some gardeners criss-cross black cotton between them for birds, but there is a danger that their legs become entangled, cut and broken. Netting is kinder.

242   There is some evidence that birds don't like the pungent smell of lavender, so placing clumps where they are most likely to peck could dissuade them. However, as birds do a marvellous service of eating slugs and insects and are just so nice to have around, putting a bird table and regular nibbles well away from cats is a particular pleasure for many gardeners.

See also 92, 93.

243   Mice won't go near peas or beans if the seed is soaked in paraffin before planting – about 30 minutes will do.

Insects

244 French marigolds are like nursemaids. Their good 'vibrations' drive whitefly from plants like roses and tomatoes, peppers and aubergines.

245 Water roses, cabbages and other delicacies which greenfly crave, with leftover washing up water to keep greenfly at bay.

246 Garlic planted round rose bushes is another age-old greenfly deterrent.

247 Alternatively, a weak soap solution applied twice a week should get rid of greenfly, provided you take care to soak the whole plant – undersides of leaves as well.

248 Solve the problem of aphids on fruit trees by growing trailing nasturtiums up their trunks. Nasturtiums also do an efficient job of bug-blasting where you have whitefly in a greenhouse.

249 Kill aphids with a cheap DIY rhubarb spray: chop 3 lbs (1.4kg) of rhubarb leaves, place in 6 pints (3.4l) of water and boil for an hour. Strain the liquid, and when cool add a solution of 1 oz (25g) of soap flakes dissolved in 2 pints (1.1l) of warm water. When well mixed, it's ready to spray.

250 A spiral of kitchen foil twisted round the roots of young cabbage plants keeps the cabbage fly from nibbling, and rows of creosoted twine, strung around their beds, will take care of air attacks.

251 Cauliflower seedlings prone to cabbage root fly will benefit from a 6 inch (15cm) protective collar made by cutting out a disc of foam carpet underlay and fixing it round the stem after planting. Slit the disc at the side, slip it in place making sure that the hole in the centre is no greater than the stem's width, which would defeat the object.

252 Outwit the carrot fly by sowing the more resistant varieties, such as Nantes and Amsterdam, in February and March and then again in June when there is less chance of a major assault. Alternatively, try pelleted seed which doesn't need transplanting or thinning – the time when carrot fly is usually attracted.

253 Tie a fresh bunch of nettles in front of open doors and windows in summer to dissuade flies, wasps etc from visiting.

254 Flies and mosquitoes hate mint. Rub a fresh sprig on your exposed parts before working in the garden.

255 Wasps for some reason are attracted to mothballs. Place some in an open trap away from the nest, to draw them out.

256   Bees and wasps can be a pain when attracted to busy gardeners who, despite trying to ignore them in the hope that they'll go away – the best policy – suffer painful stings. The easiest, cheapest and most effective remedies come from the kitchen cupboard in the form of vinegar or 'Winegar' for Wasps and Bicarbonate of Soda for Bees, to help you remember. Important that you do; if you get it the wrong way round it can make matters worse!

257   As bees and wasps tend to hang around sweet things, lure them away from you with a jam jar into which you've placed a thick honey or sugar solution, and pierced some holes in the lid with a beer can opener. This way they can crawl in, but can't work out how to exit.

258   Ants will never cross a chalk line. The age-old bait for ant traps is made by mixing 1 part sugar to 2 parts powdered borax. But where there are children and pets around, a safer remedy is to pour boiling water on their nests.

259   Beetle catching is especially appealing to children. Put some treacle or honey in a soup plate and make gangways leading up to the bait with strips of cardboard which have been rubbed over with a cut onion.

260   If caterpillars are becoming a nuisance, gather some branches of elder, cover them with water and boil them for 20 minutes. Once cooled, spray the solution on the infected plants. Alternatively, just pick them off and drown them in a bucket of water.

261   An earwig trap is made by filling a flowerpot with hay or straw and leaving it near the plant, or filling the flowerpot with moss and inverting it on top of a stick. Poke the moss out and pour boiling water over it or throw the whole thing on a bonfire to destroy the earwigs.

262 The presence of red spider mite is indicated by leaves which have become brittle and yellow-brown in colour, accompanied by a white webbing attached to the underside of leaves. An effective treatment is simply to spray the whole plant, not forgetting the undersides of the leaves with plain water.

263 A plant which has become weakened by scale insects often suffers in silence for some time as these still, brown creepies are hard to detect. But once you have identified the problem, you can remove them with much patience and methylated spirit or white spirit applied on a cotton bud.

264 Insects which invade a houseplant's soil will be killed off by a disgusting brew of cigarette butts boiled in water for 10 minutes. Strain off the ends, and leave the tobacco water to cool before watering the plants with it.

265 Make your own general purpose insecticide from milk, paraffin and water in equal quantities. It's essential to mix the milk and paraffin first; then the water can be blended in easily afterwards.

266 Ladybirds are not purely decorative. The adult munches through a hundred or so greenflies in a single day, so don't spray them with insecticide or otherwise try to remove them.

267 Mealy bugs are clearly seen, as they resemble little dots of cotton wool on the joints of stems and undersides of leaves. Rub them off plants with methylated spirit applied on a cotton wool bud.

The Handy Person's Garden

268 Look under 'Coopers' in Yellow Pages to find the cheapest barrels which, cut in half, make terrific containers for flowers and herbs. Seal the wood with yacht varnish or a timber preservative.

269 You can make attractive garden chairs from old barrels by sawing the barrel through the middle, stopping halfway, and correspondingly from top to middle, thus leaving the lower half intact, but only the half of the upper half to form a back. A circular seat of stout wood can then be nailed into place and the whole chair painted or given several thin coats of yacht varnish, with the hoops picked out in black. (See diagram.)

circular seat
nailed into
position

saw barrel
vertically
to middle

saw
horizontally
through
middle of
barrel

270   When using plastic or wooden trellis to train a rambling rose or other climber up a wall, remember the plant has to be able to entwine itself around the trellis and not just attach itself to the surface. The technique for securing it is to fix the panels 1 or 2 inches (2.5-5cm) away from the wall with cotton reels or small wood blocks. Fix them to the wall with masonry pins and nail the trellis on to them.

271   Make a large, ornamental garden table from an old door which has been stripped, weatherproofed with varnish and placed on top of pretty patterned concrete screen walling blocks cemented together.

272 Old floorboards can be cut up and made into window boxes. Use a few brass screws to secure the edges and drill drainage holes in the base. Give the outer surface a coat of plant-friendly wood preservative – not creosote – varnish or paint.

273 An ornamental fish pond is well within the realms of DIY improvements to the garden. The easiest way, once the hole is dug, is to lay a PVC pool liner, the material being specially designed for the job. Take care not to trim it too small, as the weight of the water will pull the sides down more than you think. Calculate the size by taking the greatest length and the greatest width and adding twice the maximum depth to both figures. Remember to slope the sides gently to allow small animals who fall in to escape.

See also 104–106.

274 Splits in wooden garden furniture are impossible to mend without some form of clamping whilst the glue dries. Force the split open a little to apply the glue all over the damaged surfaces before binding. To apply a tourniquet keeping the joints in place, either wrap stout string or cord round, or cut the inner tube from a tyre into rubber bands to slip over the join. To tighten, take a piece of wood, inserting it between the thing you're mending and the cord or band. Twist it round until tight and anchor it securely.

275 Where it's necessary to use a metal clamp, protect wooden surfaces with a pad made from an old rubber glove. If you do dent a wooden surface, leave an ice cube on it overnight. Cover with a tea cloth the following morning and place a hot iron on the top. This will make the dent rise.

276 Restore an old deck chair in time for the hazy days of summer. Unpick the old material. Repair any cracks or tighten loose joints using the padding and tourniquet method. Apply a coat of yacht enamel to the reinforced frame. Bind a strip of foam rubber around the bars at the top and bottom of the chair to take some of the strain off the cover. Use the old chair cover as a pattern, buying the same amount of new material (including hem width) in brightly striped canvas.

277 For the roller method, you need twice the length of the material, folding it over the bars and securing it back on itself. Free of pins and tacks it can be repositioned to save wear and tear on material, supports the weight better and is generally more comfortable.

278 People who sell you teak or cedar sheds and garden furniture will swear that they don't need extra weatherproofing, but in fact these woods look better and last longer if coated annually with a timber preservative. Always pay particular attention to the undersides and legs and feet which stand in water. Never use creosote which is poisonous to plants which may come in contact with the wood. My favourite all-round, environmentally friendly protector for garden wood, stone and even terracotta is Sylglas ClearShield from DIY shops and hardware stores.

279 To paint or varnish garden furniture (such as cast iron with scrolls or woven cane) use a spray, apply a proprietary weather resistant cover such as car paint or yacht varnish, and put plenty of newspapers underneath. Wicker chairs are heavy drinkers and need more than one coat.

280   For wicker garden furniture which has become saggy with constant use turn upside down, pour plenty of boiling salted water over it and leave to dry in the sun on a hot day.

281   Cracks in paving stones can either be opened, cleaned and filled with cement or you can lift out the damaged one and replace it. Where they are very badly cracked, get a sledge hammer and smash the whole lot, fill with cement mixture and you now have instant crazy paving.

282   To remove splashes of cement, dirty marks, or paint drips from bricks, use another brick like an eraser to rub it off.

283   It's wise to employ professional help when installing garden lighting. Modern structures use a 12 volt system which works off a transformer and is then connected to its own 13 amp fuse in your consumer unit/fuse box. To operate at mains voltage you must get the Electricity Board or a qualified electrician to do the work on outdoor equipment. Alternatively try solar lighting which needs none of this.

284   Never plant trees or shrubs so close to a house that they are hazardous in a gale; their leaves could block gutters and obscure the light to windows. If they are too close the roots can seriously damage drains and foundations. Especially in clay soil, trees such as poplar, elm and the weeping willow are among the worst offenders. Consider smaller varieties such as the purple tipped willow which is suitable for the average sized garden. As a rule, it's asking for trouble to plant a tree closer than 18 feet (5.5cm) from the house.

285   You can save considerable sums of money by knowing your legal rights. If a neighbour complains about branches from your trees overhanging into his garden, you may want to be helpful by having them removed, but you are not legally bound to do so. However, if the neighbour decides to cut them off – as is permissible – they are still yours and should be returned to you.

286   Wandering roots could cost you dearly if they cause damage to a neighbour's walls and foundations and for this you are responsible.

287   Check before lopping down long-established trees that there isn't a preservation order, protecting their right to grow. Check with your local planning authority.

Barbecues

288   Build your own with bricks, arranged in a hexagonal shape for best support, an old metal door scraper and the roasting pan from a domestic cooker.

289 A biscuit tin with a metal grid from a grill pan on top is easily portable for picnics and does the same job as a shop-bought barbecue.

290 Whatever you use as a container for charcoal, line it first with aluminium foil, shiny side up and add a layer of gravel or sand. This makes it easier to clean afterwards and reflects the heat back on to the food, speeding up the cooking process.

291 Never use volatile fuels such as petrol or paraffin to ignite the charcoal. They may be cheaper than purpose-made barbecue fuels, but they are dangerous and the fumes will ruin the taste of the food. White block firelighters or meagre amounts of methylated spirits – used with care – are cheapest, but should always be allowed to burn out before putting food near them.

292 Sprinkle a few sprigs of fresh herbs on to the charcoal at barbecue time to add to the atmosphere and give a mouth-watering aroma as the food is cooking.

Window Boxes, Hanging Baskets and Other Containers

Window Boxes

293 | Vegetable and herb growing in a window box is possible and practical too. Choose small varieties like radishes, cherry tomatoes, and add 3 onions to give green tops for snipping and flavouring soups and stews. Plant garlic cloves alongside parsley, basil, chives and marjoram, but forget mint which will take over until you can no longer see daylight out of the window.

294 | Another less conventional idea for window boxes is to have them on an inside sill with the container painted to match the decor. Plants can be kept in their containers so that they can be taken out at watering sessions, but the tops camouflaged with moss and peat when in position.

295   One snag with window boxes is that wet soil splashes on to the panes in heavy rain. A top cover of gravel around the plants will stop this.

296   Stone or even wood troughs without drainage need a good layer of 'crocks' assembled from pieces of broken flowerpots or irregular shaped stones placed in the bottom for drainage. Lay some pieces of charcoal to keep the soil sweet and a covering of peat over that. If you are potting directly into the trough, use John Innes potting compost No 2 but if the plants are to remain in their containers, simply continue to build up the peat around them.

Hanging Baskets

297   Water hanging baskets by placing ice cubes on top of the soil. This will stop them dripping everywhere.

298   Short of ice cubes? An old saucer or plastic flower pot base placed at the bottom of the cage when planting a hanging basket will help prevent floods when watering and retain some of the moisture in between times.

299   When filling a hanging basket it's important to work from the inside out, pushing plants through the sides after positioning their roots carefully from within, as you top up with soil. Pushing them through later from outside is more likely to damage them.

300   By securing hooks or brackets for hanging baskets, you can work a pulley system with a length of cord (or an old plastic-coated washing line cut in sections). Once positioned it can be locked in place to hook on a wall until it needs to be lowered for easy watering – but be sure that the point at which it's attached is strong enough to hold it when heavy with water.

301 To save time and effort when watering hanging plants, secure a bamboo cane along the last few feet of hose pipe to keep it rigid, enabling you to reach the high spots easily.

Other Containers

302 Mount groups of terracotta pots, containing brightly-coloured flowering plants and trailing ivies, on a doorstep or mellowed brick wall to bring the Mediterranean to the back door.

303 A tiered vegetable basket, when out of favour for use indoors, will store several trailing plants on a patio.

304 Tempting though it is to remove bulbs in pots and containers as soon as they finish flowering, they should be allowed to die down naturally to fully replenish the food supply back from stem to bulb. 'Dead head' them, then tidy the leaves by bending them double, and slip an elastic band over each one to keep them in place until they have turned brown and can then be removed.

305 Figs are ideal for growing on a patio in large containers as this restriction of the roots encourages a maximum crop of fruit.

306   Gooseberries can also be grown in tubs and trained up a patio wall giving easy access to the fruit.

307   To grow a grapevine you need a sunny wall and a rich compost with good drainage. But if careful attention is paid to watering so that they don't dry out, they make a most attractive cover for a pergola.

308   For both a flower and fruit plant to decorate a sunny patio wall choose a quince. Planted in good compost and trained into a fan shape it is understandably popular and provides you with a few pots of delicious quince jelly for winter breakfasts.

309   Although it is attractive and fun to grow strawberries in barrels with tiered outlets, they are less easy to water than ones planted in the top of a barrel. Solve the problem by rigging up an irrigation system using a length of plastic drainpipe with holes drilled at intervals, and insert it vertically down the middle of the barrel when planting.

310   Grow Impatiens (busy Lizzie) around home-made pillars for a riot of colour on a patio or balcony. Use a cylinder of strong wire netting lined with polythene and fill it with compost. Make holes in the polythene and insert the plants at intervals both up the sides and across the top. Once growing, a profusion of flowers will fill the gaps.

311   When planting in small spaces, whether window boxes, baskets or in tubs on patios, the simpler the layout the more eye catching the display. Avoid a cluttered look with too many varieties; stick to 2 or 3 in carefully chosen colours.

312   Unconventional containers for plants on patios include everything from the kitchen sink to chimney pots, coal scuttles and old lorry tyres painted white. A browse round junk yards pays dividends.

313 Lightweight containers such as fibreglass and plastic are preferable for roof gardens where high regard has to be given to their load-bearing capacity when heavy with water. Stone containers could seriously damage your roof.

314 A beanstalk is attractive when tied from a window box or balcony to a similar overhanging ledge above.

Making Fresh Flowers Last

Picking and Choosing

315   As with fish, Mondays should be given a miss when buying cut flowers. They will have been left over from the weekend.

316   For perfect freshness, pick flowers when half way between bud and opening in the early morning or late in the evening. Avoid the warmest part of the day as flowers gathered at their lowest moisture giving point won't last long. When buying, only select flowers which are half way between bud and being fully open.

317 Tulips should first be wrapped securely in wet newspaper up to their heads and soaked in deep water to absorb the maximum amount and stop their heavy heads bending the stems. When arranging, a pin pushed just below the head on each stem will give them extra support.

318 So that flowers get the maximum amount of moisture up to their stems without an airlock, cut off the bottom couple of inches (5cm) under water.

319 Pick forsythia in bud only, when wanted for an indoor arrangement.

320 Cut lily stems at a slant and put them in a bucket of water up to their necks before arranging. Be careful how you handle them – their bright orange pollen can stain skin and clothes.

321 Singe the bottom of poppy stems with a candle or cigarette lighter before arranging to make them last that little bit longer.

322 Hydrangeas will last longer if water is taken in through their absorbent heads first – so leave them upturned for a couple of minutes in a bowl before placing in a vase of water. Afterwards, spray daily to top up the moisture content.

323 Thirsty violets can also take in water through their heads. Stand them upturned in a bowl of water for about 30 minutes before arranging.

324 I must confess to little experience of lilac in vases having had a mother who was superstitious about bringing it indoors, but I could never find out why. It is a fact that the bark will poison the water in a vase unless peeled off before hammering or splitting the woody stalks to allow more water to soak up, to keep the heavy heads from drooping.

325 Lupins are great drinkers with literally hollow legs, and the secret in keeping them perky is to fill them up with sweetened water (one tablespoon sugar to 1½ pints/1 litre) warm water to dissolve the sugar. When full, seal the sugar in with small pieces of cotton wool pushed in on a cotton bud and let them stand up to their bottom blooms in water for at least a few hours before arranging.

326 Flowers from spring bulbs are the only ones which don't need frequent changes of water. Cut them well above the white part of the stem and rinse the white residue under the tap. Giving them a generous pinch of salt will keep the water fresh and revive them when they look like flagging.

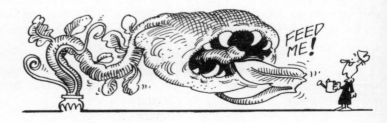

327 Always strip the bottom leaves from cut flowers before placing them in a container. Leaves left below the water level make the water slimy and smelly.

328 If taking roses from the garden, always cut to an outside leaf bud. Remove the lower leaves, strip the thorns and remove any damaged outer petals. Bash the base of the stems with a hammer to let water in. Various tests show that placing roses in lemonade really does prolong their active life.

329 All wood-stemmed flowers should have their ends crushed or split, as with roses. If they are showing signs of wilting, stand them for a short time in hot water. Split softer stems with scissors, but never scrape their outer surface.

330 So as not to damage the plant when tips and branches are removed from flowering shrubs, remove the whole shoot to within 2 buds from the old wood.

331 Anemones are very susceptible to light and heat and will open very quickly if placed under a table lamp. Use wire mesh or a pin holder to position them in an arrangement rather than oasis or sand, as they don't absorb moisture well.

332 The Flowers and Plants Association provides consumers with seasonal information about the different varieties available and how best to care for them. Their address is:
FPA
Covent House
New Covent Garden Market
London SW8 5NX
Tel: 071–720 2211

Good – and Bad – Companions

333 Add the odd foxglove to any cut flower decoration and they'll prolong the life of their companions considerably.

334 Stocks are anti-social and drink copious amounts. Keep them on their own in a large container and top up the water frequently.

| 335 | Carnations are also best kept by themselves, but are one of the longest lasting of flowers if the stems are cut between 2 nodes (nobbly bits on the stem) under water and left to have a drink for an hour or so in a bucketful of water before arranging. Bashing the stems accelerates their intake of water. |

| 336 | Keep carnations well away from a fruit bowl. Apples give off a gas harmful to carnations. |

| 337 | Don't put daffodils and tulips in the same container as this will shorten their life. |

| 338 | Nasturtiums shouldn't be added to arrangements, as they will kill off any flowers sharing a drink with them. |

Making Them Last

| 339 | Placing flowers in lukewarm salted water makes them last longer. At the first signs of fading, cutting ½ inch (1cm) from the stems and immediately plunging the trimmed ends in boiling water will get a surprising amount of extra mileage from them. |

| 340 | Spraying cut flowers with a fine spray, especially where the atmosphere is dry through central heating or stale with smoke, keeps their faces cool and lets them take in moisture through the leaves. |

| 341 | Short stemmed flowers will keep fresh for double their life if placed in a bowl of well watered sand. |

| 342 | A teaspoon of household bleach added to the water of cut flowers prevents the water becoming cloudy, but to remove a slimy film from a stained glass use bicarbonate of soda. |

| 343 | A teaspoon of household detergent added to a quart (1.1l) of tepid water will revive most jaded cut flowers and an aspirin in the water is another old favourite but, as with humans, it shouldn't be taken until needed. |

| 344 | Add starch to the water to help cyclamen, tulips and other similar stemmed flowers remain upright. |

| 345 | Orchids may seem a luxury, but are really good value as cut flowers, lasting up to 6 weeks. |

| 346 | Heathers will last for weeks without their flowers wilting or needles dropping if kept without water. Stick the cut stems into a raw potato. |

| 347 | Nipping the topmost buds from gladioli, snapdragons and delphiniums will increase their life expectancy when placed in water. Always remove the lower full-blown heads as soon as they start to fade. |

| 348 | To keep the fresh, fluffy look of mimosa, place the cut stems in hot water and spray their faces a couple of times daily. |

| 349 | Salt added to a vase of tulips will stop their heads opening fully, extending their life accordingly. |

| 350 | Toss copper pennies into the water to stop tulips from drooping. |

| 351 | If the stems of gerberas go limp, stand them up to their necks in a milk bottle topped up with water for maximum support after trimming the stem. They will soon stiffen up again. |

352 Flowers which are wrapped in cellophane and the base of their stems sheathed in damp cotton wool will stay fresh in the fridge for up to a week.

Making Them Last Even Longer

○ *Preserved flowers . . .*

353 To preserve roses for use in winter, pick the flowers just before they are in full bloom. Melt some ordinary sealing or candle wax, and wrap the ends of the stems in it. Roll in tissue paper and place in an airtight tin or box. When you want the roses, take them out in the evening if possible, cut off the waxed ends and leave them in water overnight. Next day the roses will have made the transition back to freshly cut blooms that look as if they have just been picked.

354 A single bloom will last for years if kept in a bottle or jar of surgical spirit which has a screw top lid. After the first few days, when the flower has absorbed some of the spirit, top it up and screw the lid on tight.

○ *Dried flowers . . .*

355 To keep flowers indefinitely, cut the stems short – to about 9 inches (22cm) or less – and hang them upside down in small bunches using rubber bands rather than string. Keep them in a darkish place. If preserved like this when young, they'll keep their colour once dry and look terrific in baskets and jugs.

356 Dylon dyes can be used to emphasise or change the colour of dried flowers – especially effective when preserving grasses.

357 Clean dust from dried flowers periodically with a gentle blow from a hairdryer. If really dirt-encrusted, pop them in a stout brown paper bag, add a handful of kitchen salt and give them a good shake.

○ *Pressed flowers . . .*

358 A tip from a lady who makes framed flower pictures: she keeps a supply of daisy stalks, which, after pressing, don't become brittle and break as many other varieties do and are therefore useful stand-ins.

359 You don't need to buy special weights for flower pressing. Heavy telephone directories will do nicely.

360 For speed of pressing: use an iron, protecting the flowers first inside two sheets of blotting paper, paper towelling or toilet tissue, and then placing that between newspapers. Set the iron at the temperature for pressing wool. After removing it from the newspaper, put the flowers in their blotting paper sandwich inside a weighted down telephone directory, and place in the airing cupboard overnight.

361 Make a pressed flower candle by securing the flower (with a little egg white on the back of the stems) to the candle and applying a thin coat of clear melted wax on top. Allow it to dry thoroughly. Store in the fridge for at least a few hours before lighting to ensure slow burning.

Making Arrangements

362 Keen flower arrangers cut down costs by growing their own especially for the purpose. Yarrow (achillea), the chalk plant (gypsophila), gayfeather (liatris), knapweed (centaurea) and African lily (agapanthus), phlox, golden rod (solidago) as well as dahlias, chrysanthemums, and various grasses grown for their seed heads are among the most popular.

363 You can meet up with other like-minded flower arranging enthusiasts and get lots of free advice by getting in touch with:
The National Association of Flower Arranging Societies
21 Denbigh Street
London SW1V 2NF
Tel: 071–828 5145

364 Flower arrangers know the value of white flowers – either on their own with just green foliage, or to intensify the colour of other flowers – white carnations with blue cornflowers etc.

365 Picture in your mind how you want the finished result to look before selecting the 'lead' flower which will dictate the length and height of the others. Before putting it in place, check that the visible stem length is about 1½ times the greatest measurement of the container (height for a vase, breadth for a shallow bowl). Trim and shape the others so that they are shorter by degrees, forming a pleasing shape from the central flower.

366 When you only have a few flowers, use an odd number.

367 When you want a dramatic sculptured arrangement, try a few white lilies teamed up with a selection of odd-shaped branches. The humblest tulip takes on an exotic, oriental appearance if the petals are gently bent backwards to reveal the stamens.

368 A table arrangement must complement the setting without being so high or wide that it creates a barrier with guests ducking around it to talk to each other or fishing pollen and foliage out of their food. Put foil under the table cloths to avoid marks.

369 Table flowers needn't cost a lot to look spectacular. Richly toned anemones are ideal for an arrangement, especially where it complements large dark china and table linen.

370 After a few days a flower arrangement needs an overhaul. Cut back the stem ends and stand for a few seconds only in boiling water. Follow this with a cold drink for several hours immersed to the neck. Prop them with newspapers too if needs be, before arranging.

371   Keep a store of odd-shaped branches, interesting lightweight logs, attractive shells and pebbles in a large cardboard box. They themselves will provide an eye catching design with just the addition of a few flowers.

372   An assortment of leaves and bracken placed between sheets of newspaper under much trodden rugs, will be pressed dry for beautiful arrangements of autumn colours when the garden is bare.

373   Coat berries with clear nail varnish to stop them drying out or dropping.

374   Spray unusually shaped foliage, seed pods and grasses with pewter or bronze paint from art shops for professional looking arrangements.

375   Wash and bleach magnolia leaves and use their skeletons on wires for a striking effect.

376   If your garden foliage is limited, treated selected leaves with 1 part glycerine to 2 of water and place in sunlight for a lighter colour.

377   Stems should never cross visibly and a good trick here is to make a criss-cross mesh on top of the vase using strips of sellotape.

Containers and Equipment

378   Basic props are wide-meshed chicken wire, a pin holder (a heavy lead base with sharp pins) and oasis or flower foam. Florists wire is useful for short or broken stems, but a cigar tube secured with a rubber band can be concealed in the foliage in an emergency.

379 You don't need expensive vases for flower arranging. You can do wonders with sardine cans packed with wet sand and covered with moss and pretty stones or a pin holder embedded in an odd-shaped log, or a piece of driftwood.

380 Whatever the container, it shouldn't clash with the colour scheme of your room and plain white, brown or glass containers are therefore best buys. Build up a stock of extras from jumble sales, such as china soup tureens, milk jugs and teapots.

381 A DIY flower holder can be made from a potato cut in half and placed base down so that it sits squarely, with holes pierced in it with a skewer to hold the flower stalks. Ideal for a shallow arrangement as the potato retains enough moisture to feed the plant for several days.

See also 316.

382 Drinking straws cut to the required length make useful props for short, smaller stemmed flowers.

383 Marbles in the bottom of a vase are useful for propping stems upright and, in a glass vase or bowl, are attractive too. They also give stability and, like sand, stop top heavy arrangements from tilting over.

384 Bowls and vases which can damage polished surfaces need a mat made from baize or felt and cut to the exact size of the container's base, so that it offers protection without showing.

Plants On The House

385 An old-fashioned potion enhanced the smell of flowering plants grown from seed, by soaking them for a couple of days in an infusion of rosewater and a few drops of musk oil. Once the seeds had partially dried out, they were planted in the normal way, but watered with the leftover rosewater mix.

386 Unusual though it is, worms have found their way into potted plants. Bury a slice of raw potato under the surface of the soil to draw the worms to it. Any that can't be easily removed like this will die off if the sulphur ends of matches are left stuck at intervals in the soil.

387 Bring a poinsettia into bloom again next Christmas by putting a black dustbin liner over it at night to protect it from artificial light.

388   Don't throw out extendable curtain rods; they provide the ideal support for tall plants. As the plant shoots up, you can lengthen the rod.

Buying

389   You just need the palest of green fingers to rear prolific growers in the houseplant 'easy' range. Spider plants (clorophytum), tradescantia (wandering Jew), sansevieria (mother-in-law's-tongue) and rhoicissus (grape ivy) are 4 confidence-givers for the novice.

390   However tough a species, the buyer should beware of roots popping out of drainage holes, mottled or yellow leaves or brown leaf tips and any plant which looks pale in colour and decidedly jaded. Faded labels are a good giveaway that a plant is past its sell-by date.

391   Never buy houseplants which have been sitting outside on a pavement or inside in the draught of a doorway. The ill effects may not be apparent when you make your purchase, but the plant's life could be shortened considerably from such thoughtlessness on the seller's part.

Moving and Travelling

392   A plant which is being moved from outside to in (and vice versa if it's cold outside) will acclimatise better if the plant and pot are put in a transparent plastic bag for a few days.

393   For protecting small potted plants when travelling or leaving them outside at night, try cutting the bottom halves from plastic lemonade or coke bottles. They will fit surprisingly well on top of the pots in many cases.

Positioning

| 394 | Never move a plant once it's doing well in a certain spot, but turn it round regularly for even growth; otherwise it will lean towards the light. |

| 395 | Only keep houseplants on window sills at night in winter if there are blinds. Window areas that are shut off by curtains will kill plants by trapping cold air around them. |

| 396 | If you're given an African violet, but don't have the sunny windowsill which they love, keep it under a tablelamp and leave the lamp on at night. |

Feeding, Watering and Cleaning

| 397 | A few drops of castor oil fed to the soil every 6 weeks will make house plants greener. |

| 398 | Try the water from boiled eggs (when cooled) on your African violets and watch them bloom from the added calcium. |

| 399 | Rinse milk bottles with water and pour on houseplants to provide free plant food. |

| 400 | To improve the colour of plants which have become pale and anaemic-looking, add a teaspoon of Epsom salts, preferably to rainwater, for their next drink. |

| 401 | When it's snowing, fill buckets with the stuff. When melted to room temperature this will provide a houseplant drink full of health-giving minerals. |

402 Invest in a water butt – even a couple when sales are on. Rainwater is the cheapest and by far the kindest tonic for plants.

403 Water your plants with leftover tea. They will benefit from the boiled water and the fact that it's tepid. Stone cold water chills plants.

404 Brown-tipped leaves are often an indicator that chlorine in the tap water is adversely affecting houseplants. If you can't change to rainwater, at least allow the tap water to stand overnight before applying it.

405 A simple test to gauge if a plant needs watering is to leave a pebble on top of the soil. If, when you turn the pebble over, it's damp on the underside the plant has plenty of moisture; if the pebble is dry, it needs a drink.

406 Practised nurserymen test with a thumb on the soil, to see if it feels springy and therefore is holding enough moisture. If it's unyielding to the touch, it's too dry. A skewer placed in the soil – near the rim so as not to damage the roots – should come out with a little moist soil adhering to it if there's sufficient water in the compost.

| 407 | Plants with fleshy stalks such as pepperomia, cyclamen and African violet must never be watered from on top or the stems will rot at soil level. At watering time, stand their pots in 2 inches (5cm) of water until you can see moisture glisten on top of the soil (half an hour should be enough). It does no harm to water other delicate plants by this method for safety's sake.

| 408 | Is there a sadder sight than a collapsed cyclamen? It could, hopefully, just be crying out for a good drink. Stand it on an upturned teacup in the middle of a bowl to make a moat and keep its feet dry. Make a stout paper collar to wrap around the stems so they are protected and then you pour boiling water in the bowl. The steam rising up will revive it.

| 409 | It is absolutely vital that azaleas should never be allowed to dry out, and there's a very good moisture gauge on the wooden stem between soil and shoots. Look for a dark water mark, roughly half way up the stem. If the mark is higher, up to where the branches begin, it is too wet, and if there's no mark at all, it's too dry. Always check this before home watering and never buy a plant where the indications are that it is too wet – or worse, too dry.

| 410 | Give houseplants an occasional tonic by watering them with sooty water.

| 411 | The majority of plants need to rest between September and April to store up their energies for the next season, so it's important during this dormant period that you don't try to force them to keep going with plant food and overwatering. No food and very little watering is the rule until they show signs of regrowing in spring, and don't feed flowering plants when they are in full bloom.

| 412 | Make your own plant food by grinding calcium rich egg shells with roughly an equal amount of caster sugar, and add this mix to the soil.

| 413 | A teaspoon of ammonia in 1½ pints (1l) of water, is a nursery favourite to push on the growth of plants. Ferns will stay a healthy bright green when given this mixture occasionally.

414 Don't throw leftovers of wine or beer down the sink; mix them with a little water and give the plants an intoxicating drink to perk them up considerably.

415 It can't be said too often how much plants prefer sweet rainwater, but a little vinegar added to the watering can before filling up with tap water will at least act as a water softener, neutralising the chalk content. Cooled, boiled water from the kettle and fizzy mineral water gone flat are also free from impurities and preferable to tap water.

416 As many plants die from too generous watering as too little, but a shrivelled up specimen, with gaps between earth and pot rim which is gasping for moisture, needs drastic action. Stand the pot in enough lukewarm water to cover it completely and, unless it's a hairy leaved variety, sponge the leaves with a little water of the same temperature to which a little milk has been added. In a couple of hours you should see a marked improvement.

417 Plants which have become water-logged, can occasionally be saved by removing them from their containers and standing them in a makeshift 'pot' of tissue, blotting or newspaper in a warmish spot to absorb as much of the damaging excess water as possible.

418 As a general rule, water in the morning between mid-September and May and not late in the day in cold weather as the drop in temperature overnight could severely chill the roots.

419 Don't spend money on expensive leafshine for plants. Polish them with skimmed milk – never olive oil as some recommend for rubberplants etc, which only clogs the pores and attracts the dirt.

420 Save coffee grounds and tea leaves for mixing with houseplant compost. Ferns will be especially appreciative.

421 Ferns were greatly prized in Victorian parlours. Housemaids kept them clean and fresh by placing them in the bath tub every 2 or 3 weeks and washing them with a mild soap and tepid water solution.

Planting and Potting

422 Mix charcoal pieces with soil at the base of plant pots. A good way to use up those leftover bits from summer barbecue packs and it acts as a ventilator to stop compost becoming soggy and sour.

423 To efficiently repot a plant, take the pot in which the plant is already growing and place it inside the one into which the plant is to go. Pack the compost tightly into the space between the pots. Remove the inner pot, carefully remove the plant from it and place it in its immaculately tailored space and firm round.

424 If a plant sticks when you are trying to get it out of a pot, try a push from underneath with a pencil through the drainage hole.

425 Speed up the start of date and peach trees by soaking the stones for a couple of days in a cup of water.

426 Halves of grapefruit skins filled with compost make good beds for indoor seedlings.

427 Plastic flowerpots can be an eyesore unless placed inside more decorative containers, but old gramophone records, gently heated at the edges so you can mould them into a bowl shape with wavy edges, make unusual pots for bulbs or arrangements. They also have the advantage of a built-in drainage hole in the middle.

428   If you don't have pots to spare, put moist compost in a transparent polythene bag, insert seeds, pips or stones in the soil and tie the bag securely. Put the bag in the airing cupboard until shoots appear.

429   Propagating cases are an unnecessary expense. Put up to 6 stem cuttings (depending on how big they are) into a well scrubbed pot of peaty compost. With a couple of sticks in the soil, make a tent by covering the pot with a polythene bag and keep them at no less than 16°C (60°F).

See also 18.

Plants for Free

430   Take cuttings from an overgrown rubber plant to provide luxury presents for friends at little cost to you. Strip a piece of bark from around the stem 8 inches (20cm) from the top of the plant. Cover this stripped section with a ball of moist sphagnum moss, wrap in clingfilm and secure to make an airtight polythene bubble. In a few weeks, roots will have established themselves in the moss, and it's time to snip the cutting clean from the bark and pot it in compost.

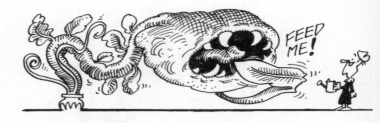

431   Free plants can be grown from pips and stones such as the avocado pear. Soak the stone in warm water and remove it from its outer covering. With its pointed end up, stick 3 toothpicks into the sides of the stone so that it can now perch on the rim of a wide-necked jar with its base in water. Keep the water level topped up. Pot when roots are developed.

432 Orange, lemon, tangerine and grapefruit provide indoor trees. Wash the pips and plant 3 or 4 to a small pot in sandy compost. In summer put them outside to make the wood harden.

433 Collect 'free' seeds from the plants growing in your garden. On a dry sunny day, select only ripe seeds – those which have, in most cases, gone from green to brown – together with capsules and pods, and spread them on newspaper in a warm, dry place to persuade them to open and release their contents.

434 For a pineapple plant, slice off the crown and plant the fleshy disc in a sand-based compost, or even in a saucer of water. They need lots of light and warmth and will die in less than 18°C (65°F).

435 When carrots are bought with fresh fern-like crowns, slice the tops to leave about half an inch of base to place on their own or in between spindly or bare stalked plants for instant foliage or ground cover.

436 Never handle seedlings by the stems or you'll bruise them. Use a pointed stick to loosen the earth around the roots and then use the stick as a lever under the leaves to lift.

437 You will increase the life expectancy of potted plants if you remember that sand makes soil lighter but lets plants dry out more quickly, and that peat increases the soil's capacity to retain moisture. A mixture is ideal. Plants in porous terracotta pots need more frequent watering than those in plastic pots. Plastic containers are more likely to become waterlogged if the plant is given more than it needs to drink.

438 The choice of plant pots will very much depend on your pocket and whether you want to disguise them in a outer container. If proper attention is paid to its drinking habits the plant itself

has no preference. Placing a plastic or clay potted plant into a decorative container, always put a layer of pebbles at the bottom of the outer pot first, on which to stand the plant for drainage. It's easy otherwise to water, and not notice that the inner pot is standing in a puddle. Plants hate to get their feet wet and cold.

439 Garden soil is really only suitable for garden plants, and won't do for seeds and young greenhouse plants that need the kind of nourishment and sterile conditions they can only get from potting compost. Garden soil also tends to breed pests and disease in vulnerable seedlings.

440 When planting geraniums, add coffee grounds to the compost to increase growth.

441 Date stones will germinate in moist compost with their pointed ends upwards and just level with the soil which must be kept damp and in a warm dark place (airing cupboard) until shoots develop, after which time the 'date palm' can be introduced to the light.

442 An African violet always makes a welcome present. Collect small brown bottles, ideal because they keep out the light. Take a fully grown leaf, cutting cleanly, leaving about 3 inches of stalk. Allow it to dry out for about 2 to 3 hours. Fill the bottle with water, cover it with a small piece of kitchen foil and fit that snugly over the top of the bottle. Pierce a hole *just* large enough for the stem to go through into the water. In the few weeks it will take for roots to appear, you'll have to top the water level up if necessary.

443 Other fleshy succulents such as the popular jade or money plant (crassula argentea) and gloxinias, pepperomias and begonias, can all be propagated successfully by the leaf cutting-in-the-bottle method, but a useful tip to stop them 'bleeding' is to first dust them with charcoal powder.

444 When growing new geraniums from old, they will actually benefit if the cuttings are allowed to lie quietly for a few hours so that the surface dries and a callus starts forming. If you get a good strong pelargonium (geranium) you can nip off all side shoots for cuttings, and thus turn the mother plant into a standard. Supported with a stick, the plant will grow to 4 feet (1.2m) and can then be encouraged to bush out on top.

445 Apart from rigging up polythene bags over small pots, if you don't have a propagating tray you can grow cuttings in jars. Put 2 inches (5cm) of moist, peaty compost mixed with sand in a jam jar and put cuttings in this. To avoid too big a build up of condensation, pierce a few holes in the lid, before putting it back on, and leave in shade for a couple of days.

446 Sansevieria (mother-in-law's-tongue), the toughest of plants, is easily multiplied by cutting the leaves into sections with a very sharp knife then planting each section with one end stuck in moist compost in a pot. Remember this plant will stand anything but overwatering.

447 Begonias are easy to propagate by leaf planting/vein cutting. Select a fully developed leaf with prominent veins and with a sharp knife or razor blade make a few small cuts in the bigger veins on the underside. Shiny side up, place the leaf on damp potting compost. Weight it gently with small stones. Cover the pot with clingfilm and put it in indirect sunlight. The cuts will develop roots, and after shoots form and the plants are big enough to be independent, pot them on.

448 It's possible to save quite a bit of money raising your own houseplants from seed and have plenty over to give as presents at little extra cost. Asparagus ferns, African violets, the begonia rex and coleus would give the novice grower a nice selection to start with in the spring. For Christmas, the Christmas cherry (solanum capsicastrum) with bright red berries and the red pepper (capsicum annuum) can be raised from seed.

Pests and Diseases

449 Greenfly seem greatly attracted to begonias and other tasty houseplants. A clove of garlic embedded in the soil will ensure that the attraction is short-lived.

450 When a plant has a pest infestation, isolate it and spray with a solution of soap and water which could do the trick without resorting to pesticides.

451 Sickly plants, if they're going to die, go downhill fast. It's often best to salvage the top and treat it as a cutting before it's too late.

Orchids

452 Orchids won't stand overwatering – once a week from above is more than enough. After watering, always return a potted orchid to the same position on the windowsill to ensure that the flowers on the spike are facing in the same direction.

453 To achieve the humidity which orchids need, stand them on trays of wet gravel, but as you don't want them to soak up water from below, slip plastic lids or jam jar tops underneath the pots, but just above the surface of the gravel.

454 There are special orchid fertilisers, but if you have difficulty finding one, use a liquid fertiliser at half strength, and an ordinary houseplant food at full strength is OK in the summer months.

455 The cymbidium or boat orchid is the easiest variety for the beginner to grow and the most popular in the shops for Christmas flowering. It enjoys being outdoors from June to September, even if the temperature is a bit lower than the seasonal norm, but won't stand intense heat or the sun's glare so put it under a tree or even on a balcony with dappled shade.

Plants Are 'People' Too

456 It's an established fact that plants respond better to owners who talk to them and stroke them. If you're still not convinced, take 2 identical species of young plants from cuttings. Give one the special treatment daily and not the other. The one that is stroked and has nice things whispered in its ear will, in a short time, look sturdier.

457 Tip from a well-known Dutch flower grower – never thank someone for a plant as if it's an inanimate object – you'll hurt its feelings and it won't do well for you.

458 Plants like company: keep them in groups and spray above them very lightly to help them build up their own greenhouse atmosphere.

Bottle Gardens

459 In September, when many houseplants benefit from being cut back, you can experiment with cuttings to make a bottle garden. Avoid fast growing plants such as tradescantia and rhoicissus. A good slow growth mix would be calathea (peacock plant) Saint Paulia (African violet) aphelandra (zebra plant) and cryptanthus, which looks like a star fish.

460 You don't need expensive containers from florists for bottle gardens. Use spotlessly clean wine or cider flagons, sweet jars or carboys and line the bottom with pebbles and charcoal for good drainage before adding compost through a funnel. Use a fork and spoon firmly strapped to bamboo canes, or tongs to position and bed in the plants. A razor blade on a bamboo cane trims off damaged leaves.

461 A cork or cotton reel securely attached to a stick, or impaled on the pointed end of a knitting needle, is good for firming in the soil once plants are in position; they need to feel securely anchored in the compost for the root to spread.

When Away

462 When you go on holiday, soak a thick bath towel with water and leave your well watered houseplants sitting on this. They will absorb just enough water to keep going. Don't stand them *in* water as the roots will become waterlogged and rot. (Wet newspapers, although more messy, will do as well). Filling the bath with enough water to just cover a layer of bricks on which you need to stand the plants, also gives them all the moisture they need.

463 Small potted plants can be well watered and placed inside perforated transparent plastic bags, sealed at the top and placed in as cool and shady a spot as possible to contain water loss.

464　When you're away for just a few days and want to leave plants in situ, put damp pebbles around the top of the soil to prevent evaporation of the moisture underneath. (Gravel or moss will do as well.)

465　Denuding window sills of plants is often a good indicator to burglars that you have gone on holiday. Some plants such as sansevieria (mother-in-law's-tongue) actually thrive on neglect and appreciate drier conditions while acting as visible watchplants in your absence.

466　Garden thieving is on the increase, which has prompted the manufacture of burglar-proof hanging baskets. It's worth having a word with your local crime prevention officer for advice on protecting lawnmowers and other tempting portables when you are away from home.

Indoor Bulbs

467　Some of the prettiest containers for indoor bulbs – such as ceramic bowls – become porous when accidentally cracked through constant use. To cure this, clean the bowl and dry it thoroughly. Place a candle stump inside the bowl and place it in a warmish oven until the wax melts and can be swirled around to coat the base and up to two thirds of the sides. Take

care, however, not to overheat the oven or you could risk a
further crack in the container. Put a wedge of newspapers
underneath the bowl in the oven as an insulator for safety's
sake. When cold, the wax coating will have made the bowl
waterproof.

468 When planting bulbs in indoor containers, fibre is cheaper
than compost but in the long term if you want to move them to
the garden or save them for another time, a good potting
compost is an investment.

469 You actually don't need fibre or compost at all to give a splash
of colour and a heavenly scent from a single hyacinth for a
bedside locker or an office desk. To grow a hyacinth in a glass,
buy the biggest bulb you can find and fill the glass with
rainwater preferably, until it almost touches the base of the
bulb. Add a few pieces of charcoal to keep the water clean.
Place the glass in a cool dark room until the sprouts grow to
about 3 inches (7.5cm) high, then gradually introduce it to
brighter light. It's important to keep the water topped up to
the original level.

470 Buy bulbs for Christmas flowering before the end of September. Choose prepared or pre-cooled specimens, the largest
and firmest, and plant them immediately after buying them.
Forced bulbs can't be grown in bowls indoors for more than
one season, but can be moved to the garden thereafter. To
prevent them becoming over-dry, they can be wrapped in
aluminium foil and stored in a box or suitcase meantime.

471 Don't be tempted to plant more than one type of bulb in each
bowl; otherwise they'll bloom and fade at different times and
completely spoil the whole arrangement.

472 Before planting tulips, peel off the brown skin, taking care not
to damage them as they bruise easily.

Saying It With Flowers

473 Sending flowers is always a gamble. The customer finds (from Yellow Pages) a teleflorist or member of Interflora and places the order, often by telephone and giving a credit card number. The florist nearest the address of the recipient then takes the order and, *unless instructed otherwise*, will make up an arrangement as she likes, to the value of the order.

474 Be specific where you can, regarding how many roses, chrysanthemums or whatever are required and always ask for flowers which are at their most plentiful and cheapest at the time of delivery. For instance roses are superabundant in summer, but out of season are not only expensive but of inferior quality.

475 You can send flowers to almost any country abroad but in this case you *should* leave the choice to the florist delivering them as you will not necessarily know what is in season there. The trick when sending abroad is to place your order weeks in advance if possible. It then goes by letter saving expensive telephone and telex charges.

476 It is sometimes difficult to complain about poor quality or bad service when given flowers as a gift, but rather than risk upsetting the sender you can write to the following addresses if the florist concerned is displaying their sign.

Interflora   British Teleflower Service Ltd
Interflora House   146 Bournemouth Road
Watergate   Chandlers Ford
Sleaford   East Leigh
Lincolnshire NG34 7TB   Hampshire S05 37B
Tel: 0529 304141   Tel: 0703 265 109

477 Vases in hospitals are scarce and the finding and filling of them takes up valuable time on the part of the hospital staff. Better to take a locker arrangement using a plastic tub weighed down with pebbles, damp sand and a little oasis for support. Cover the container in kitchen foil.

478 Take a lead from florists who deliver to hospitals and go for sweet-smelling flowers in pretty pastel shades – freesias, sweet peas and doris pinks are among the favourites. Least popular are – stark red and white combinations; too funereal, or a continuation of the blood and bandages theme perhaps.

Selling Your Wares

479   If you mean to take up selling your wares for a living, Barty Phillips' *Plants for Profit* (Piatkus Books) goes into all aspects in detail with suggested available courses, marketing techniques, legalities, income tax and VAT problems, which plants to grow and when etc.

480   When making out a catalogue – it can be as simple as a sheet of paper advertising your wares – always give the Latin name of plants as well, for easy identification.

481   Join your local gardening club or flower society; you might well find a suitable partner to combine resources, give moral support or just to cover each other to allow for unexpected illness, time off for other duties and holidays.

482 Remember the old adage 'Time spent in reconnaissance is seldom wasted'. Do your homework, visit the opposition, know the current rates and aim to give a better service and top quality product for slightly less money.

483 If you have carpentry skills, consider making window boxes and garden furniture. Hand-crafted goods, at less than the large retail outlets charge, can be made to order at a workbench in the garage and samples displayed on your lawn.

484 Position your water butt close to your working area to save time when potting and watering your produce.

485 Much easier to be an expert on one species, whether cacti, orchids, heathers etc, than to try to learn something about everything. Ask a large specialist nursery to recommend courses and books, then build your own collection of healthy breeding stock. Apart from selling their offspring, you may be able to write articles or give talks to local organisations. Your fame (and free advertising potential) will soon spread.

O *Vegetables . . .*

486 The temptation is great these days to grow 'organic vegetables' and sell them for much more than the common or garden cellophane-packaged ones. Before a product can be described as organically grown, the grower must be a registered member of the Soil Association, who will test your soil and advise you. Their address is:
Soil Association
86 Coleston Street
Bristol BS1 5BB
Tel: 0272 290661

○ *Herbs . . .*

487 Herbs either in pots, in bottles of vinegar and oil or dried (see 180) and attractively packaged, are popular at agricultural shows and craft fairs, especially when your range extends to pretty herb 'sleep' pillows. Local advertising and a sign at your garden gate would help you get started.

○ *Cut flowers . . .*

488 These are usually sold from your door, or try to persuade local florists, village Post Offices or greengrocers to take them. Put up a sign at your garden gate when you have a glut and stand them in deep containers of water with their feet wrapped in cotton wool and most important, keep them in the shade. Never let cut flowers stand in the rain. Try your nearest hospital to ask if you could bring a supply for visitors.

○ *Fruit . . .*

489 Place a sign at the garden gate and try taking samples to local shopkeepers, making your rates as competitive as possible; or make up attractive baskets for a delivery service. Local advertising, unless for a personal delivery service, is less successful when you have competition from pick your own fruit growers in the area.

○ *Plant arrangements and hanging baskets . . .*

490 Start with an amazing display outside your home to catch the eyes of passers by. Have leaflets printed and pop them through doors at the time when flowering plants are re-emerging. Have an album of photographs to show examples of how you would make up baskets, their colour schemes, prices etc. Offer to take empty baskets for refilling to cut down cost to customers. Grow plenty of fuschias, lobelia, dwarf sweet peas, trailing geraniums and variegated ivies etc. Display at craft fairs, car boot sales and agricultural shows where, if you look up the prospective exhibitors, you may get orders for other stands.

○ *Plants for offices . . .*

491 Write to the person in charge, ask for an interview and show samples and arrangements. Be business-like about what you will offer in the way of maintenance contracts and prices. Keep to a reasonable radius or you will soak up the profits on time and petrol getting around to tend everything. Start with your own bank manager, building society, local hotels, pubs, health clubs etc.

○ *Smellies . . .*

492 Lavender sachets, pot pourri, rosewater etc. Emphasise the moth repellent properties of lavender as well as scenting drawers and wardrobes. Recipes for pot pourri and rosewater – (*for recipes see 142, 143, 144*) – go well with lavender, and rosepetal sachets too, for a popular cottage industry. Craft fairs a must, car boot sales, health shops, gift shops and advertising at Christmas.

○ *Gardening services . . .*

493 One of the biggest garden pests is the jobbing gardener who has the temerity to offer his or her services, without having much to offer in the way of expertise. Make sure you can back up your claims to be in charge of someone else's precious garden – perhaps using your own as a showpiece – or else stick to offering lawn cutting, digging vegetable gardens and general tidying up. Put cards in shop windows in areas where people can afford to pay for help. If you're good you'll be inundated with offers of work once word gets around.

○ *Garden designing . . .*

494 Landscape architects/planners are skilled people who charge small fortunes on the basis that you should recover the cost of their fee when you come to sell your house. There is some scope for the amateur who has ideas, has made a go of their own or friends' gardens and who offers to do work to owners' specifications at more reasonable rates. Make up photo albums, catalogues, and have cards printed – displaying them in local shops. Contact a local newspaper reporter who might be persuaded to do a piece about your own garden and how you'd be glad to help others.

○ *Flower arranging . . .*

495 Post leaflets through doors to the kind of hostesses who get in outside caterers when entertaining. Try hotels and look in the anniversary and engagement columns – try to get business for weddings etc, by placing an advertisement nearby.

○ *Dried flowers . . .*

496 Usually displayed in pretty baskets, lace trimmed posies etc. Try door-to-door leaflets, craft fairs, personal visits to owners of beauty salons and larger hairdressers, and advertisements, especially at Christmas time. At craft fairs sell either bunches, made-up arrangements or separate loose varieties for people who want to make up their own. Also sell copper containers, ceramic jugs, painted baskets etc.

○ **Pressed flowers . . .**

497 These can be used for greetings cards, bookmarks, candles etc. (*See 358–361.*) Learn how to do your own picture framing or pick up bargains from jumble sales. Buy cheap wooden ones which can be painted. Sell at craft fairs.

○ **Preserves . . .**

498 Lemon curds, marinated fruits, pickles, chutneys, hampers. Start with a good cookery book which specialises in traditional farmhouse-type recipes. Then, unless you mean only to supply to friends or on some other informal selling basis, you would have to conform to regulations regarding the sale of food, its packaging and labelling. Get advice from your local weights and measures authority. Once established, you could sell to tea-shops and delicatessens as well as at craft fairs and from your own kitchen door with a sign at the gate.